Guide to Getting a Federal Law Enforcement Job

Career Advancement

Internships and

Entry Level Positions

About the Authors

Michael Grace was born in upstate New York. He received a Bachelor's of Science degree in Marketing from the University of South Florida in 1988. In the same year, following the steps of his father and grandfather, he began his federal career with the United States Customs Service. After assignments in Vermont and at the preclearance Customs' Port in Toronto, Ontario, he transferred as a Supervisory Inspector (Instructor) to the Customs' Academy in Brunswick, Georgia. While there, he was detailed to the Physical Techniques Division of the Federal Law Enforcement Training Center (FLETC) and eventually switched federal employers from the Customs Service to FLETC. With FLETC, he has held a number of progressively challenging positions including; Law Enforcement Senior Instructor, Law Enforcement Program Specialist, and currently serves as a Supervisory Law Enforcement Instructor (Division Chief) in the Training Management Division.

What qualifications does the author have regarding federal law enforcement hiring?

- Michael Grace has 32 years of federal law enforcement experience.
- He is a committee chairperson for recruiting and retention at the Federal Law Enforcement Training Center, the nation's largest trainer of federal law enforcement officers.
- He has first line supervisory experience with law enforcement Special Agents and uniformed police officers from the Secret Service, Marshals Service, Capitol Police, Central Intelligence Agency, Customs Service, Customs and Border Protection, Immigration and Customs Enforcement, Fish and Wildlife Service, National Park Service and many other federal agencies.
- He has vast experience with vacancy announcement rating and ranking panels, writing position descriptions, writing and designing job interview questions as well as interviewing federal job applicants.
- He has worked at the FLETC since 1992. Each year, he literally sees tens of thousands of law enforcement students from the various federal agencies that pass through the doors of the consolidated training facility.
- For three years, he was a coordinator of the FLETC's College Intern Program. He and two others organized the various aspects of the intern program from writing the interview questions, and conducting telephone interviews to making the final intern selections.
- He has helped develop, modify, and revise basic and advanced training programs for most of the major federal law enforcement agencies in the United States.

C.J. Ross was born in Maryland. He joined the US Army Military Police Corps in 1983 and was stationed at Fort Riley, Kansas and Grenada, West Indies. He received his Bachelor of Arts degree in Criminal Justice from the University of Maryland in 1987. In the following year, he began his federal civilian career with the United States Park Police with assignments in New York City, Washington DC and San Francisco as a patrol officer, field training instructor, criminal investigator, horse mounted officer, and sergeant. In 1997, he transferred as a Sergeant (Supervisory Instructor) to the US Park Police Academy in Brunswick, Georgia. While there, he was detailed to the Physical Techniques Division of the Federal Law Enforcement Training Center (FLETC). In 1998, he received his Master of Science Degree in Criminal Justice Education from Troy State University. In 2000, he switched federal employers from the US Park Police to the Bureau of Land Management as a State Staff Ranger in Reno, Nevada. In 2002, he transferred to the FLETC. With FLETC, he held a number of progressively challenging positions including: Law Enforcement Senior Instructor and Law Enforcement Program Specialist. In 2005, he transferred to the Fish & Wildlife Service where he served as a Chief Ranger and Supervisory Law Enforcement Instructor (Branch Chief) for the National Wildlife Refuge System. In 2010, he transferred to the Federal Law Enforcement Training Accreditation Board as a Program Manager. In 2018, he retired after 32 years of service to become the Director of the Park Ranger Law Enforcement Academy and Minnesota POST Academy at Vermilion Community College in Ely, Minnesota.

What qualifications does the author have regarding federal law enforcement hiring?

- C.J. Ross has 32 years of federal law enforcement experience.
- First line and mid-manager supervisory experience with law enforcement Special Agents and uniformed police officers from the Secret Service, Marshals Service, Capitol Police, Central Intelligence Agency, Customs Service, Customs and Border Protection, Immigration and Customs Enforcement, Fish and Wildlife Service, National Park Service and many other federal agencies.
- Vast experience with vacancy announcement rating and ranking panels, writing position descriptions, writing and designing job interview questions as well as interviewing federal job applicants.
- He worked at the FLETC since 1994. Each year, he literally saw tens of thousands of law enforcement students from the various federal agencies that pass through the doors of the consolidated training facility.
- For two years, he coordinated the Bureau of Land Management's Student Careers Employment Program in Nevada.
- He helped develop, modify, and revise basic and advanced training programs for most of the major federal law enforcement agencies in the United States. This includes field training evaluation programs, first line supervision, and middle managers.

Foreword

Law enforcement is a noble profession. Some have likened officers to knights in the medieval ages. I prefer the analogy of officers as Sheppard dogs that protect the flock of sheep from the wolves. While these philosophical comparisons are interesting, the bottom line is that law enforcement officers are expected to intervene in hazardous situations, often times moving toward danger when others are running away. Police officers are expected to use lethal force on a suspect when necessary. If moving toward danger or using lethal force is not something you can do because of religious or other reasons, then police work is not for you.

More than ever before in the history of mankind, timely and accurate information is of immense value. Some of the information gathered in this book is taken directly from government Web pages and reports that are available to anyone free of charge through the Internet. In fact, where appropriate there are Hyperlinks to applicable references and Web sites. While the World Wide Web is an amazing resource, making sense of the vast quantity of information is difficult at the very least. This guide is of value because it provides the reader with timely and accurate information and an insiders' understanding rather than gigabytes of useless information available through indiscriminate Internet searches. The information provided explains federal law enforcement employment so that a layperson can understand and use it to help find the right federal law enforcement job.

We live in a society that all too often expects immediate gratification and quick fixes to problems. This phenomenon could be labeled the lottery mentality. The reality is that good things in life are usually a result of much groundwork and sweat equity while the bad things in life often happen fast and furiously. I mention this as a reminder that reading and applying the advice provided will not guarantee or automatically enable you to get a federal law enforcement job. Be wary of anyone that promises that for you. Education and experience take time and these may be two of the most important pieces of the puzzle for getting the job you want.

In writing this guide, it is my intent to provide you with information about the **unequal** federal law enforcement job choices in much the same approach as a mentor or trusted advisor. I promise to be sincere and straightforward to try to guide you toward the right job while providing you with my insider's perspective of how to get that job. I will present information to assist you in making federal law enforcement career choices as well as present you with advice to increase your odds of success when applying and interviewing for federal law enforcement jobs and internships. It is certainly best to have the knowledge contained in these pages early on in your career rather than later; however, even the seasoned federal officer will find insightful and useful information in these pages. After reading and going to the Internet links in this guide, you will have a much clearer understanding of the complex and often-confusing world of federal law enforcement jobs.

Table of Contents

Chapter 1: Introduction

When it comes to federal law enforcement, not all jobs are created equal. If you are looking at federal law enforcement as a career that could easily span the next 10, 20, or 30 years, you owe it to yourself to find the best possible job. In a decade old survey conducted by the Office of Personnel Management (OPM), they ascertained that most newly hired federal employees found out about their new job from a friend or relative. With the exponential increased usage of the Internet over the last few years, I am sure the statistics have moved in favor of the World Wide Web as the main source of information for federal jobs. However, in either case, by friend or Internet, it is unlikely you will get the whole picture on federal law enforcement jobs without some inside the fence guidance.

Unfortunately, there is little uniformity from one agency to another so advice given by someone without a broad knowledge base will likely be of limited value. In fact, I have found that many current federal law enforcement employees have very limited knowledge on their own agency's hiring process. Consider this: two jobs may be virtually identical in the actual tasks that are done by the employee yet one offers a higher salary, double the money for retirement, and enables you to retire ten years sooner. In some cases, annual leave (vacation time) and certain retirement benefits will not transfer to another federal agency should you decide to switch federal employers.

With so many different federal agencies and job positions, how do you know which are the right fit for you? Chapter three of this book will go into that question in much more detail but for starters, do your homework. The Internet is a valuable tool to check out the various agencies. I prefer a more personal perspective and suggest talking to police officers to get their opinions. If you do not know any federal officers, most state and local law enforcement officers will have worked with the federal officers in some capacity and can offer their view on the subject. Keep in mind that opinions, including mine, are highly dependent upon perspective. Beauty is truly in the eye of the beholder.

Understanding and applying good job securing techniques, tactics, and strategies, will help increase your odds of landing the law enforcement position you want. Most persons applying for federal jobs make the mistake of mass mailing their resume to any vacancy announcements. This type of shotgun approach to job hunting can sometimes be effective for entry-level positions but usually ends up with high hopes dashed by long waits and no response. The shotgun approach is a lot like playing the lottery. A better method is to have a rifled approach that is very focused and limited in scope.

Many job seekers that have had poor success with the application process will fall into the resume rewriting trap. These unsuccessful applicants try to write and rewrite the "perfect" resume they think will get them the job. My experience is that a resume can open or close a door but it is not what gets you a seat at the dinner table. Be sure to read Chapter 11 for the real deal on resumes. My suggestion for anyone seeking their first appointment to a federal job is to read this guide in sequence from beginning to end then go back to the various Internet Hyperlinks for more detailed information if necessary.

One of the most important concepts to understand for someone seeking a federal law enforcement job is the definition of a law enforcement officer. To most people, the definition of a law enforcement officer is someone with the authority of the government that carries a gun and enforces criminal laws. If only it were that simple! OPM's definition covering most new employee's states: A law enforcement officer is an employee whose primary duties are the investigation, apprehension, and detention of individuals suspected or convicted of offenses against the criminal laws of the United States.[1] The Federal Employees Retirement System (FERS) definition also includes employees primarily performing "investigation, apprehension, and detention" duties who transfer to supervisory and administrative positions and employees who have "frequent and direct" contact with convicted criminals, such as prison support staff. Unfortunately, under this definition, many federal police jobs are not classified as law enforcement for the purpose of retirement.

6C (Pronounced – six C) is the common jargon used to describe an OPM recognized law enforcement position.[2] A "covered" position is another description you may hear and it means the same thing as 6C. A "non-covered" position refers to a job that is not under the 6C retirement. The positions that meet the 6C definition of law enforcement have special advantages regarding minimum retirement age and retirement annuity (pension).

The only disadvantages are a mandatory retirement at age 57 and a maximum age limit (usually 37) for hiring[3]. Some jobs such as Capitol Police Officers have retirement systems that mimic 6C; however, there is a difference. Technically speaking, Capitol Police Officers are in a covered position; however, they won't receive 6C credit for time served in the Capitol Police should an employee switch to an actual 6C law enforcement position.

Federal law enforcement positions come in all different shapes and sizes and for someone new to the game or to the uninformed; the process of getting the job you want can be quite confusing. The definition of what is and what is not an OPM law enforcement position is a perfect example of the confusion. It is human nature to try to categorize things to make sense out of the chaos and confusion. I prefer to think of the different law enforcement positions as fitting into one of three categories; internships, entry level jobs, and career advancement positions. All three of these types of positions have similarities; however, there are also some unique differences.

---

[1] http://www2.opm.gov/oca/leo_report04/part_ii.asp#b
[2] The term 6C comes from the special retirement provision for law enforcement officers and firefighters found in section 8336(c) of title 5, United States Code.
[3] There are exceptions to the mandatory retirement age and the maximum age upon entry.

The reality is there are many different, yet correct, categorizations of federal police jobs. Depending upon perspective, some of the other ways to view federal police jobs are:

- 6c Law Enforcement Covered vs. non-covered
- Merit vs. All Sources, and Other
- Competitive vs. Noncompetitive
- Executive/Legislative/Judicial/Other
- CSRS vs. FERS
- General Schedule vs. Pay Banding vs. Other
- Military vs. Civilian
- Full-Time Equivalent (FTE) vs. Term vs. Temporary
- Journeyman vs. Entry Level
- Uniformed vs. Plain Clothed
- Eighteen-elevens vs. O-eighty-threes and others.

If those different categories do not make much sense to you right now then no worries, read on. Let's start with the basics.

Basic Terminology

Every industry has their own language with acronyms and words that have special and specific meanings. Federal law enforcement is no different. The glossary at the end of this book has a comprehensive list that will help you understand the federal law enforcement human resource vernacular. Throughout this book, the terms law enforcement officer and police officer are interchanged and meant to describe the general meaning by a lay person: A law enforcement officer is a person who carries a badge and a gun under the authority of the government. It is very important to understand the OPM law enforcement definition is not the same. The Chapter on Retirement and Other Benefits will provide the specific differences between 6C and non-covered positions.

The list that follows includes essential definitions necessary for you to understand the rest of this book and the proper use of the words will enable you to converse intelligently with recruiting officers and human resource personnel. You will find the word "competitive" is somewhat overused by the federal government as demonstrated in the definitions that follow. My only explanation is there must have been some real problems in the past with selecting friends and relatives for government jobs and the Feds now try to market themselves as being fair and open...competitive. Reading two pages of definitions is dry stuff. It is unavoidable, have patience.

- Appointment - An appointment is the official act of saying "You're Hired." A person can be selected for a position and months later be appointed. Typically, this time delay is due to background investigations and other administrative delays. Other occupations would use the terminology; ordained, knighted, or crowned instead of appointment. There are several types of appointments, which convey different rights.

- Assessment – Examination, rating and ranking, and assessment all mean the same thing. It is an evaluation of an applicant, where each person is assigned a numerical score.[4]

- Best-Qualified List – a certificate for a competitive hiring authority.

- Certificate – also known as a list of eligible candidates. It is a paper document listing the eligible candidates. OPM or agency human resource personnel usually give this document to the hiring officials. The same document is given back to OPM or human resource personnel after the selecting official and approving official indicate the person(s) selected for the position.

- Civil Service – This means civilian government employment as opposed to military employment. There are two types of civil service, Competitive Service and Excepted Service. Each conveys different employment rights.

- Competitive Examination – A hiring authority used in conjunction with an All Sources Vacancy Announcement to select applicants in which the persons are evaluated (examined) and given a numerical score from which a rank order (highest to lowest) is derived.

- Competitive Hiring Authorities – this usually refers to All Sources Competitive Examination and Merit Promotion hiring authorities. These hiring authorities have a best-qualified list.

- Filling a vacancy - the process of advertising, and selecting someone for a job.

- Full-Time Equivalent – is uniformly known by the abbreviation FTE. It is a permanent position or job. When the abbreviation FTE is spoken, it is pronounced as the singular alphabetic letters FTE rather than trying to make an acronym out of it.

- Hiring Authority – an approved method or process, which allows an agency to hire someone. Law, regulation or executive order establishes hiring authorities.
- Hiring Officials – There are normally three hiring officials: a recommending official, selecting official, and approving official.

---

[4]There is another type of assessment that is rarely used where there are large groupings of applicants rather than an individual score. I have never seen this system used in law enforcement hirings.

- Knowledge, Skills, and Abilities – also known by the abbreviation KSAs. They are topics that an applicant writes a narrative, usually 1-2 pages, which are graded by officials. The grade or assessment is used to decide if the applicant makes the best-qualified list.

- Merit Promotion – A hiring authority used in conjunction with a Merit Promotion Vacancy Announcement to select applicants in which an alphabetized certificate of best-qualified candidates is provided to the hiring officials. Noncompetitive Hiring Authorities – sometimes referred to as alternate staffing methods. These are methods used to hire employees in which the applicants must meet some minimum standards or qualification requirements but applicants do not vie against each other based on examination/assessment scores. These hiring authorities offer selecting officials the most latitude on who they pick. Appointments made under noncompetitive hiring authorities are in the Excepted Service, albeit in some cases temporally.

- Position - a job or more specifically a certain type of job, e.g., Special Agent, Border Patrol Agent, or Capitol Police Officer. Each position series has a number assigned to it. For example; all Border Patrol Agents are numbered 1896 (pronounced eighteen-ninety-six), all Special Agents are 1811 (pronounced eighteen-eleven). In addition, each position has a written position description that identifies duties and functions of the job.

- Selected - The act of being chosen by a selecting and approving official. A selection is to an appointment as an engagement is to a marriage. When someone is selected, it does not necessarily mean they have the job. Typically, a background investigation and medical/drug screening test must be favorably completed.

- Special Agent, Criminal Investigator, or 1811 all mean the same thing. These are law enforcement officers that investigate criminal activity. All Special Agents meet the OPM definition for law enforcement officers covered by 6C retirement.

- Vacancy or opening - a job position that has not been filled. For example; when an employee retirees, his or her leaving the work force provides the agency with a vacant or open job that can usually be filled with another person.

- Vacancy announcement - the advertising or posting of a job opening that is intended to be filled.

Competitive Service and Excepted Service

It is important to know that all federal jobs fall into one of two different human resource systems; Competitive Service or Excepted Service. We all remember from our high school days there are three branches of the federal government; Executive, Legislative, and Judicial. What you may not know is that OPM falls under the umbrella of the Executive Branch and is sort of a centralized human resources organization. OPM oversees the Competitive Service human resource system for the Executive Branch agencies.

Competitive Service jobs are subject to the civil service laws passed by Congress to ensure that applicants and employees receive fair and equal treatment in the hiring process. The Competitive Service laws also provide for workers' rights against adverse actions such as being terminated from employment. This does not mean you cannot be fired for performance or conduct issues, it just may take longer. Like many laws passed by Congress, the Competitive Service laws do not apply to their own Branch of government (with the exception of the Government Printing Office). In fact, neither the Legislative nor Judicial Branches are in the Competitive Service; therefore, all of the law enforcement jobs in the Legislature and Judicial Branches of the government are Excepted Service positions, e.g., Capitol Police and Supreme Court Police.

Excepted Service positions are not subject to appointment, pay, and classification rules in Title 5, United States Code. Although not required to do so, agencies in the Excepted Service often use hiring processes similar to their Competitive Service brethren. Seems simple enough, right? Not so fast. Specific agencies/departments within the Executive Branch are in the Excepted Service; the Central Intelligence Agency, Federal Bureau of Investigation and State Department are examples.

The reasoning behind this is that some executive service organizations are so closely tied to national security or presidential policy the executive branch (the President) needs greater control to hire and fire people without the restrictions imposed by the Competitive Service. Lastly, positions (as opposed to agencies) may be in the Excepted Service by law, by executive order, or by action of OPM.[5] The best example of this are persons appointed under certain hiring authorities like the Outstanding Scholar[6], or Student Educational Employment Program. Employees appointed under some special hiring authorities are temporarily in the Excepted Service and can sometimes be converted to the Competitive Service after a brief period. The significance of the Competitive Service versus the Excepted Service in your job choice is important and discussed further in Chapter 2.

---

[5] http://help.USAJobs.opm.gov/jobseeker/jobsearch/
[6] OPM advised agencies to no longer use the Outstanding Scholar Program as of November, 2007.

Types of Appointments

As touched upon earlier, an appointment in government human resource language does not mean a meeting. It is more like the official blessing of a person to be an employee. In most cases you are selected for a position with the federal government through one of several types of appointments differentiated by length of time in the position and the type of service (Competitive or Excepted). It is sometimes easier to understand the types of appointments by thinking of them as a caste system.

The type of appointment you hold determines your benefits such as promotions, pay increases, health and life insurance, retirement coverage, and reinstatement eligibility. Reinstatement eligibility is your entitlement to get back into a Competitive Service job once you have left. It also affects which vacancy announcements you can apply under.

	Competitive Service	Excepted Service
Permanent	**Career**-Full benefits with reinstatement eligibility for life. **Career Conditional**-Full benefits package with reinstatement eligibility for 3 years.	Full benefits but no reinstatement eligibility.
Term	Greater than 1 year but less than 4 years in length. Appointment may be terminated by written notice. Eligible for within grade increases, retirement coverage, health and life insurance. No reinstatement rights or promotions.	Greater than 1 year but less than 4 years in length. Appointment may be terminated by written notice. Eligible for within grade increases, retirement coverage, health and life insurance. No reinstatement rights or promotions.
Temporary	Appointment made for 1 year or less but can be extended for one additional year. No benefits (health or life insurance, retirement coverage, or within grade increases unless in the wage grade pay system.)	Appointment made for 1 year or less but can be extended for one additional year. No benefits (health or life insurance, retirement coverage, or within grade increases unless in the wage grade pay system.)

- Temporary Appointments: Temporary appointments are used to fill short-term employment needs of a Competitive Service agency. Temporary appointments are made for periods not to exceed one year but may be extended for one additional year. Temporary appointments may be terminated at any time upon written notice. Temporary employees in the General Schedule (GS) pay system are not eligible for promotions or within grade increases temporary employees in the Wage Grade (WG) pay system are eligible for within grade increases. Employment under a temporary appointment does not confer eligibility for reinstatement.

- Term Appointments: Term appointments are normally used to fill temporary employment needs for a project with a Competitive Service agency. Term appointments are made for a period of more than one year and may be extended up to 4 years. The appointment may be terminated at any time upon written notice. Term employees are not eligible for promotions but are eligible for within grade increases, retirement coverage, and health and life insurance. Service under a term appointment does not confer eligibility for reinstatement.

- Excepted Appointments: Excepted appointments are used to fill all of the positions in the Excepted Service. What may seem strange is that excepted appointments are also used under specific hiring authorities to fill positions that would otherwise be in the competitive system. Some examples of this are persons selected under the Student Temporary Employment Program (STEP), Student Career Experience Program (SCEP), Veterans Readjustment Authority (VRA), and the Americans with Disabilities Act (ADA) hiring authorities. Excepted appointments can be either permanent or temporary. Excepted employees under permanent appointments must complete a 1 year trial period.

- Career Conditional Appointments: A career conditional appointment is a permanent appointment in the Competitive Service that leads to career tenure after completion of 3 years of continuous time on the job. Career conditional employees are eligible for promotions and within grade pay increases, health insurance and other benefits. Under a career conditional appointment, you must complete a 1-year probationary period (sometimes longer). Generally, career conditional employees may not be promoted, reassigned, or transferred until 3 months after their initial appointment. Employees who do not have veterans' preference or who did not complete 3 years of continuous service, and who leave their government jobs while under career conditional appointments have reinstatement eligibility for 3 years from their date of separation. Therefore, without competing with other candidates, they may be reemployed to a position for which they qualify, at the same grade, or with no more promotional potential up to that of a position the employee previously held on a permanent basis under a career conditional appointment, even though the employee never reached the full performance level of the career ladder. Employees who have veterans' preference and serve any period of time under their career conditional appointment have reinstatement eligibility for life.

- Career Appointments: Employees who have completed 3 years without a break in service under career conditional appointments acquire career tenure and are converted to career appointments. If they leave the federal service as career employees, they have reinstatement eligibility for life.[7]

There is shared frustration amongst many federal supervisors regarding restrictive regulations in the day-to-day management of their employees. However, one of the few decisions managers actually should take full responsibility for is the hiring of subordinate employees. In fact, hiring decisions are arguably the most important aspect of a supervisor's job. There are also many creative ways to hire the right employee. Unfortunately the most common hiring authorities used to hire employees, All Sources and Merit Promotion Vacancy Announcements, are very mechanical and restrictive.

Competitive hiring authorities have a rigid process which quantifies the applications. The assessment scores will in reality exclude many persons from being hired by limiting who the selecting official may choose. Because of the restrictive nature in competitive appointments (Merit Promotion and All Sources hiring authorities) the use of noncompetitive hiring authorities such as internships is becoming more favored by Agencies. With the loss of the Outstanding Scholar hiring authority in November of 2007, internships will likely become more extensively used for hiring entry level positions.

As a hint of things to come in future chapters: For those of you out of school, don't let the word "internship" scare you away. Under President Bill Clinton it had a new meaning and was not necessarily associated with college. There is probably a good joke in there somewhere although the comment is serious as you will find out when reading about FCIP Internships.

---

[7] http://www.ntc.blm.gov/leadership/orientation/chapter_05.htm

1. Agency has opening	2. Hiring authority	3. Vacancy announcement
4. Applicant meets minimum standards	5. Rate & rank applicants	6. Applicant certificate issued
7. Interview	8. Selection	9. Job offer

Legend for Flowchart

1. Agency Has Opening – The generic hiring process identified in the flowchart is diagrammed for the Competitive Service. Although Excepted Service agencies are not required, many use processes that are similar to those used in the Competitive Service. Also, keep in mind the federal employment hiring process is a somewhat impersonal system. As evidence, I submit the process of hiring a new employee is universally known in the industry as "filling a position." It all starts when the agency has a vacant position[8].

2. Merit/All Sources/Alternate Staffing Authority – Agency hiring officials decides which hiring authorities they will use with advice and guidance from their human resource personnel. This decision is usually based on trying to get the best person for the job given certain constraints such as time and money. The agency can choose to open the job search very wide. In these situations, the vacancy announcement will usually indicate that it is open to all United States Citizens twenty-one years or older. This type of opening is specifically referred to as an All Sources Vacancy Announcement. In contrast, agency officials may choose to open the job search very narrow so that only certain federal employees can apply. This is known as a Merit Promotion Vacancy Announcement. Also, the selecting official may decide to use alternate staffing methods. Usually an alternate staffing method will require a vacancy announcement such as a Merit Promotion Vacancy Announcement even though the agency has no intention of selecting anyone that applies to that vacancy announcement. Often times an agency will pursue many avenues at once using All Sources, Merit, and alternate staffing methods in the hopes of having many highly qualified persons to choose.

3. Vacancy Announcement – All Sources and Merit Promotion Vacancy Announcements are usually advertised on USAJobs at http://www.USAJobs.opm.gov/. Advertising the job opening on USAJobs satisfies the requirement the agency make public the notice of intent to hire someone for a vacant position. Most people don't know there are other systems used for this public notice such as AVUE.COM. Agency Web sites will usually specify exactly where to find their publicized vacancy announcements. It is important to understand that if you are interested in employment with an Excepted Service agency, you should contact that agency directly as they are not required to advertise vacancy announcements.

---

[8] There are exceptions to the general rule that an agency must have a vacant position. One such exception is double encumbering.

4. Applicants Meet Minimum Qualifications – After the closing date or specific date listed in an All Sources or Merit Promotion Vacancy Announcement, all of the applications are compiled and checked to verify that applicants meet the minimum qualifications.

5. Rating and Ranking – All Sources and Merit Promotion applicants that meet the minimum qualifications are then put through an examination process to determine which applicants are highly qualified. The examination process could involve any number of different yet acceptable methods.

6. Certificates Issued – The names of applicants applying under noncompetitive hiring authorities that meet minimum qualifications are placed on a list in alphabetical order. Highly qualified Merit Promotion applicants names are place in alphabetical order as well. The best-qualified names of applicants in the All Sources Competitive Examination hiring authority are placed in rank order on a certificate. Note there is a separate certificate for each hiring authority and grade level. The certificates are sent to the selecting officials.

7. Selection Assessment Interview – A selection interview is not mandated by OPM regulations or any law, sometimes an agency has an internal policy requiring the interview. Selection interviews are time consuming and difficult to rate or score.

8. Applicant Selected – A selection is made when a selecting official and approving official sign a document indicating the candidate they have chosen.

9. Tentative Offer of Employment – A tentative (conditional) job offer can then be made to the applicant. The purpose of the conditional offer is to ensure the applicant is still interested in the job prior to commencing the lengthy and expensive process of medical/drug testing and investigating. Typically, for promotions, there is not a formal conditional offer as the candidates are current on their backgrounds and other requirements.

10. Medical and Drug Test Successfully Passed – Medical and drug tests are usually conducted by contracted professionals. The drug test is known affectionately as the whiz quiz and may be the only test in this process that is not helped by studying or practice.

11. Background Investigation – The background investigation usually begins after the medical exam and drug test. The length of time required to complete the investigation is dependent upon the number of other persons in the process of getting their backgrounds checked, the number of investigators available to do background checks, as well as other factors such as the type of clearance required for the position, e.g., secret or top secret. This is a lengthy process, often many months.

12. Background Cleared – Agency officials are given a background investigation report and if everything goes well, the selected applicant is given a final job offer.

13. The selected applicant is then officially appointed. There is no monarchy in the United States so it will not be necessary to kneel before the Queen; however, there is usually swearing or confirming an oath of office.

14. The appointed person becomes a new employee on the date they enter On Duty (EOD). The new employee receives a salary or hourly wage that starts when they EOD and continues during basic training.

15. Employee Successfully Completes Training – Most federal law enforcement positions have a mandatory basic training completion requirement.

15b.Some agencies will recycle some employees that fail out of training, most will not. Attitude goes a long way in this decision. Agencies are usually required to recycle students that do not complete training due to medical issues.

16. Employee Works at Duty Station – After the completion of basic training, the new employee usually goes directly to their assigned office or duty station.

17. The process repeats itself.

Chapter 2: Who Are The Feds Looking For?

Throughout my career with the federal government, I have met far too many people with great qualifications that became frustrated, disgusted, and even angry regarding the federal hiring system. After trial and failure, many good applicants simply put up their arms and say: "Who are the Feds looking for?" The federal government, like any employer, is looking for job candidates that possess traits to help their agencies excel in their organizational missions. For entry-level positions, agencies generally focus their attention on a few baseline qualities. These law enforcement baseline traits are:

- honesty,
- integrity,
- physical abilities, and
- mental aptitude.

Regarding the general baseline qualities; as you look more closely at them, you will find that each agency has their own standards for measuring and grading these criteria. The perfect candidate for an entry-level law enforcement position would:

- have never been arrested/convicted,
- have honorably served in the military,
- have demonstrated personal financial responsibility.
- liked by coworkers,
- articulate,
- athletic,
- fluent in a foreign language,
- skilled with Microsoft software (Windows, Word, and Excel),
- have a strong work ethic (shows up on time, rarely calls in sick),
- have a four year college degree, and
- usually scores in the top ⅓ of class on written tests.

Some of the requirements listed are legitimate and bona fide. However, these represent my own hypothetical preferences and are not necessarily the requirements of any agency. In fact, it would be a challenge to find many applicants who have all the qualities listed. If you happen to have all of those qualities, you will probably have many job offers and can be selective with the agency and position you want because you are a highly sought rare commodity. As the job positions move away from entry level toward the realm of career advancement, agencies expect the job applicant to have certain specific knowledge, skills, and abilities. For example, knowledge of federal court procedures, skill in conducting complex investigations, or ability to lead multi-agency task forces. Given the fact that very few people have all the qualities an agency may desire, the challenge for any applicant is to positively differentiate themselves from the other applicants.

Best Qualified

In most but not all federal job vacancies, the government attempts to quantify and rank the quality of job applicants through various examination processes. Some of the criteria may even include items on the previous page. Now let us imagine there was actually a way to truly calculate (examine) an applicants' quality, the resultant graph of all the applicants for a particular job would likely look like the bell shaped curve below. There would be a small proportion of best-qualified candidates to the far right and the bulk of applicants would be grouped toward the middle. Unfortunately being in the middle does not get you a job offer.

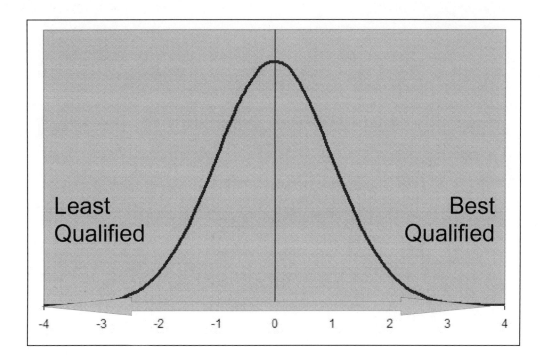

Most of us, by the very nature of statistics, will never truly be the best qualified for a job. Fortunately, for the average applicant there is no way for the government to accurately measure an applicant's true quality. In addition, there are some hiring methods that do not necessarily attempt to pick out the best-qualified person for the job. By following the advice offered in this guide, you will improve the odds of attaining the federal law enforcement job you desire. Unfortunately, like most good things in life, it can take time for the job offer to come.

Supply and Demand

The laws of supply and demand play a critical role in determining who is hired as a law enforcement officer for a particular agency. It is understood the demand for federal law enforcement jobs is far greater than the number of jobs available. Yet, it is also true that not everyone wants to become or is eligible to become a federal law enforcement officer. Because the government has a limited amount of positions to fill and an overwhelming number of people wanting the jobs, agencies can be selective on whom they choose. Each individual agency and even positions within an agency can have their own selection requirements although many of the minimum requirements are similar in nature. These requirements usually include; citizenship & residency, age, driver's license, written tests, interviews, medical exams and psychological tests, physical tests, work experience, education, and background suitability and security. Completion of basic training is usually also listed as a condition of employment. Unfortunately, there is little uniformity in the specifics of these requirements and this creates confusion for job applicants.

The cause for the variations in the basic job requirements are mostly a supply and demand issue. For example, in an applicant's background, a certain amount of illegal drug use may be acceptable to one agency while the same usage will be a disqualifier for another. In general, the less glamorous and lower paying positions are more tolerant on their background suitability requirements. One prestigious agency required their Special Agents be citizens of the United States and disqualified persons that claimed a second country for citizenship. Arguably, dual citizenship is an espionage/loyalty issue; however, that agency missed whole generations of employees that could have provided critically needed foreign language skills at a difficult time in our nation's history. Many requirements tend to be on a sliding scale that can change over time. For example, Because of recruiting problems, in 2007 the FBI relaxed their limits on disqualifying illegal drug use.[9] The following is a brief description of the common minimal requirements for most federal law enforcement jobs.

Citizenship & Residency

Almost without exception, federal police jobs require applicants to be a United States citizen. Additionally, the FBI may require that you denounce your citizenship to other countries if you are a dual citizen (Dual citizenship was previously a disqualifier for the FBI).[10]

---

[9] http://www.usatoday.com/news/washington/2007-08-01-fbi_N.htm
[10] http://www.fbijobs.gov/61.asp

Residency requirements are a somewhat new phenomenon. The bureau of Customs and Border Protection (CBP) has a residency requirement that applies to all applicants other than current CBP employees. If you are not a current CBP employee, CBP requires that for the three years prior to filing an application for employment, individuals meet one or more of the following primary residence criteria:

- Applicant resided in the United States or its protectorates or territories (short trips abroad, such as vacations, will not necessarily disqualify an applicant); or
- Applicant worked for the United States government as an employee overseas in a federal or military capacity; or
- Applicant was a dependent of a United States federal or military employee serving overseas.[11]

Age Requirements

Many federal police jobs have a minimum and maximum age level requirement. The minimum age requirement is mainly justified for maturity reasons. The maximum entry age is used in positions where it is necessary to have a young and vigorous work force. There is a rigorous duty standard established by law (5 U.S.C. 8401(17) (A) (ii)), which provides that covered positions must be sufficiently rigorous that "employment opportunities should be limited to young and physically vigorous individuals." This provision effectively mandates that an individual must pass maximum entry age and physical fitness and medical standards to be hired as a law enforcement officer. The regulatory definition of "rigorous position" at 5 CFR 842.802 requires agencies to establish such standards.[12]

- Minimum Age - Nearly all federal police jobs have a minimum age requirement of 21 years old. The FBI has a 23-year age minimum.
- Maximum Entry Level Age - Many federal police jobs have a maximum age upon entering on duty of 37 years old. Park Police has set the maximum at 31 years old. If you are over the age limit, recognize there are many gun carrying federal police jobs that have no maximum age limit. However, the jobs without an age limit do not qualify for special law enforcement retirement.

Driver's License

Nearly all federal police jobs require applicants to have a valid government (state, territory, province) issued driver's license. From my experience in a training Division responsible for teaching police driving skills to most new federal law enforcement officers, I can tell you there are a surprising number of people from major metropolitan areas who have very limited driving experience and may even have gotten their driver's license just so they could get a federal law enforcement job. If you fall into that category, I recommend getting as much routine driving practice behind the wheel of a mid to full

---

[11]

http://cbp.gov/linkhandler/cgov/careers/customs_careers/officer/officer_factsheet.ctt/officer_factsheet.doc
[12] http://www.opm.gov/oca/leo_report04/part_ii.asp#c

size car as you can prior to your academy training. Most police academies expect at least a nominal level of driving proficiency upon arrival. Jumping right into emergency response driver training without basic driving proficiency is setting you up for failure.

Written Tests

There is always an examination (assessment) of some type for competitive vacancy announcements. The examination is often a yes/no, true/false, or multiple choice written test but could be a scoring of the persons experience through knowledge, skills, and abilities (KSAs) written narratives or questionnaire. Entry-level positions are more likely to use the written test method while career advancement positions usually use the KSA written narratives or a questionnaire as the examination methodology. Only a few federal agencies use yes/no, true/false, or multiple choice written tests for promotional purposes. Assessments such as the Border Patrol Agent Exam and the Treasury Enforcement Agent Exam are examples of entry-level written tests. In my opinion, the written tests provide a low degree of predictive validity that is they are not reliable at indicating an applicant's ability to perform the actual law enforcement work. Agencies do like to use written tests because they are easy to measure and quantify and they provide individuals with a differentiating numerical score. Other types of examination are also problematic with regard to validity. In the Chapter titled Techniques, Tactics, and Strategies, I describe how you can use the different examinations/assessments to your advantage.

Interviews

Interviews are a very important component for most every law enforcement job. Interviews may be done as part of the examination or selection process and are used to differentiate candidates. Interviews are also done for the background suitability and security process although these interviews are usually a pass or fail decision rather than creating a hierarchy of applicants. An entire Chapter of this book is dedicated to Interviews and there is advice on interviews in Techniques, Tactics, and Strategies.

Medical Exams and Psychological Tests

Nearly all agencies have minimal requirements regarding medical issues such as hearing and eyesight but that is not the case when it comes to psychological testing. Many agencies just do not use psychological tests. However, through the background suitability and security process, those agencies that do not have independent psychological testing still maintain the ability to "weed out" persons that are psychologically unfit for police work. The good news for a job applicant that has made it to medical exam process is they have likely been given a conditional offer of employment. The condition is of course, successfully passing the medical exam, psychological test, and in some cases a selection interview. The conditional offer basically means the agency is seriously considering you for employment. Do not pack your bags and sell the house in anticipation of moving for the new job. Medical requirements are pass or fail as opposed to a point value system used to rank job candidates. There are a surprising number of people who make it this far only to fail because of medical requirements.

Medical requirements are an area where there are wide variations in acceptable standards. What may be a perfectly acceptable level of vision for one agency may be unacceptable for another. For example: ATF Special Agents must meet uncorrected distant vision of at least 20/100 in each eye, and corrected distant vision must test 20/20 in one eye and 20/30 in the other; however, Coast Guard Special Agents have no uncorrected vision requirements, but like the ATF their eyesight must be correctable to 20/30. The Secret Service requires Special Agent applicants to have uncorrected vision no worse than 20/60 binocular; correctable to 20/20 in each eye.

Most medical exams are administered by doctors' offices that are contracted by the government rather than by applicants' personal doctors. Unfortunately, in some cases the level of service and reliability of government-contracted doctors may not meet your expectations. I know of a recent Border Patrol Agent applicant who horribly failed his government contracted uncorrected vision test. In fact, he failed so badly the results indicated he should not even be driving a car. This was the first time this person had ever heard that news, he had never had the need to wear eyeglasses or contacts before. Thankfully, the agency had the forethought to allow him to present other medical evidence to the contrary of the agency administered eye test and the truth of the matter was that this applicant's vision was fine and the first test results were unreliable.

Usually an agency's medical requirements are available to the public on their Web site. Be sure to check the medical requirements prior to getting to the conditional offer phase so as not to waste your time and the agency's time by going through all the previous steps only to find out you are unsuitable for the job. Other medical tests commonly include blood pressure, hearing, depth perception, peripheral vision and the ability to distinguish shades of color. Many agencies have specific requirements for persons that have undergone corrective eye surgery.

Debilitating diseases are usually an automatic disqualifier.[13] Given the fact that agencies have wide variations in medical requirements, if you have a specific medical issue, my advice is to shop around for the right agency based on published agency medical standards. In other words, do not waste your time applying for an agency position that has a medical standard you know you cannot pass.

In an agency sponsored psychological test, the agency is the client rather than the person being evaluated. With psychological testing, agencies are generally looking for emotional stability, proper judgment, impulsiveness, honesty and integrity, conflict resolution, assertiveness and other social behaviors in the hopes of identifying persons that are likely to be good police officers and those that may not be good at police work.[14][15] While there is no studying for psychological tests, the best advice is to answer honestly and do not try to read-into the questions to find the answers you think are wanted. I have known people that have "failed" their police psych test with an agency and these same persons have gone on to successful careers with other agencies. If the psych tests were very reliable, every agency would be using them.

The Minnesota Multiphasic Personality Inventory (MMPI) is the most prevalent psychological examination utilized by law enforcement agencies. The test is used for determining secret and top-secret clearance suitability required for many positions within federal law enforcement agencies. The series of questions are designed to identify those poorly suited for law enforcement. Suitability is represented by their responses demonstrating a variety of counterproductive behaviors including a lack of initiative, unwillingness to follow rules, argumentativeness with their supervisors, untrustworthiness, and over aggressiveness.

Physical Tests

Physical testing and fitness testing are synonymous. However, medical tests differ from physical tests in that physical tests measure the applicants' ability to perform certain body movements, actions, or physical tasks. Some agencies use physical testing as a ranking tool while others use it strictly as a pass or fail requirement. Some have no physical testing at all. Physical requirements are near and dear to my heart since I worked extensively with a Customs Service project to establish physical standards for Inspectors and Canine Enforcement Officers. In addition, I worked as a Law Enforcement Physical Techniques Instructor responsible for administering FLETC's Physical Efficiency Battery (PEB). The PEB is a physical test that some agencies use as a pre-employment fitness standard. Specific examples and more information are provided on physical tests in Chapter 8.

---

[13] http://www.ncis.navy.mil/downloads/NCIS_Special_Agent_Applicant_Infobooklet.doc
[14]

http://www.emich.edu/cerns/downloads/papers/PoliceStaff/Police%20Personnel%20(e.g.,%20Selection,%20%20Promotion)/Law%20Enforcement%20Hiring%20Standards.pdf
[15] http://www.policepsych.com/revision_process.html

Work Experience

There are many entry-level law enforcement positions that do not ask for prior law enforcement experience; however, the more prestigious and sought after Special Agent positions usually require specific investigative experience. For example, the Secret Service requires that Special Agent applicants have three years of work experience in the criminal investigative or law enforcement fields that require knowledge and application of laws relating to criminal violations, or an equivalent combination of education and related experience.

Non-qualifying law enforcement experience is as follows: Experience as a uniformed law enforcement officer where the principal duties consisted of investigations and arrests involving traffic violations, minor felonies, misdemeanors, and comparable offenses; or in which the major duties involved guarding and protecting property, preventing crimes, and/or legal research without the application of investigative techniques.[16] It is worth noting that previous work as a federal, state, or local uniformed police officer, will usually on face value be a positive on an applicant's resume although it may not qualify as "investigative" for the purposes of work experience.

Education

Special Agent positions, regardless of agency, normally require applicants to have a Bachelor's degree from an accredited university. Some agencies are even more specific and express their desire for applicants to have majored in accounting, law, criminal justice, forensics or some other highly desired area of expertise. Nearly all federal police jobs require a high school diploma or equivalent. Given the accessibility of postgraduate degrees through distributed learning, it has become commonplace to see applicants with advanced degrees. Be forewarned that government employers are now checking the college accreditation status of selected applicants. Diploma mill degrees listed on a resume will likely permanently damage your federal job prospects.

Background Suitability and Security

I include drug testing, polygraph examination and personal investigation in the category of background suitability and security although arguably they could be separate items. Agency requirements on what constitutes an acceptable background seem to have the greatest variation of all the minimum requirements. Know this: A background check is a substantial part of the vetting process to determine if someone should be a law enforcement officer. The background investigation is used to get a federal security clearance. Male applicants that have not registered for the Selective Service are not employable in the federal government. Obviously, persons convicted of violent crimes and other felonies are weeded out early in this process. As an example of background suitability and security requirements the FBI employment disqualifiers are:

- Conviction of a felony

---

[16] http://www.secretservice.gov/opportunities_agent.shtml

- Use of illegal drugs in violation of the FBI Employment Drug Policy (see the FBI Employment Drug Policy for more details)
- Default of a student loan (insured by the United States Government)
- Failure of an FBI administered urinalysis drug test
- Failure to register with the Selective Service System (for males only)
- Conviction of a misdemeanor crime of domestic violence

There is a sliding scale for less serious issues. In determining unfavorable suitability most agencies will look at financial irresponsibility; drug/alcohol abuse; arrest history; misconduct in prior employment; association with individuals involved in illegal activities, e. g., drug use, trafficking, etc.; demonstrated lack of honesty and integrity in providing complete and comprehensive information about current and past behavior which may be unfavorable.

Almost all federal police jobs require a drug test, usually through urine analysis. A positive result for illegal drugs will usually be an automatic disqualification. However, the past recreational use of marijuana is not normally an automatic disqualifier, particularly the further in the past it occurred. "Increasingly, the goal for the screening of security clearance applicants is whether you are a current drug user, rather than whether you used in the past," said Tom Riley, a spokesperson for the White House Office of National Drug Control Policy. "It's not whether you have smoked pot four times or 16 times 20 years ago. It's about whether you smoked last week and lied about it."[17] Agencies may vary widely on their disqualifying drug use policy.

For informational purposes, in 2008 the Naval Criminal Investigative Service Special Agent position had the following standard for past drug use:

- An Applicant who has used any illegal drug while employed in any law enforcement or prosecutorial position, or while employed in a position which carries with it a high level of responsibility or public trust, will be found unsuitable for employment.
- An applicant who is discovered to have **misrepresented** his or her drug history in completing the application will be found unsuitable for employment.
- An applicant who has sold any illegal drug for profit at any time will be found unsuitable for employment.
- An applicant who has used any illegal drug other than marijuana, within the last ten years or more than three times in one's life will be found unsuitable for employment.
- An applicant who has used marijuana within the past three years or more than 15 times in one's life will be found unsuitable for employment.[18]

I like how the word "misrepresented" is used instead of "lying." Establishing that an applicant misrepresented himself or herself requires a lower burden of proof than proving

---

[17] http://www.usatoday.com/news/washington/2007-08-01-fbi_N.htm
[18] http://www.ncis.navy.mil/downloads/NCIS_Special_Agent_Applicant_Infobooklet.doc

they lied. Let us just call it lying. The reason that lying is such a critical factor is because an officer's credibility is paramount in the successful prosecution of crimes. Specifically, if an officer has been found to have lied or misrepresent himself or herself to get the job, the veracity of his or her testimony under oath will be highly suspect and likely of no value to the court. If an officer's future testimony is of no value, an agency has no reason to have that person on the payroll as a sworn police officer.

A personal interview with an investigator is a normal part of the background check and many agencies use a polygraph examiner for this process. Although polygraph results are not admissible in court, they are legally used for employment purposes. Polygraph results indicating areas of deception can also be used by background investigators to help determine areas that need greater scrutiny. Once a background investigative report is completed, it will be forwarded for review to agency hiring officials. Background investigative reports can usually be classified into three groups, sort of like battlefield triage.

- Squeaky Clean backgrounds – These people reap the rewards of clean living and get to move right along to the next step, usually a final job offer from the agency.
- Dead on Arrival (DOA) backgrounds – These people have serious background problems such as a misdemeanor conviction for domestic violence[19], lying under oath, felony convictions, outstanding warrants, and drug addictions. Others in this category are much less serious although they have fallen into the arbitrary sliding scale of automatic disqualifiers. For example; under the FBI's revised drug policy, applicants are disqualified if they have used:
  - Any illegal drug, other than marijuana, within the past 10 years or used marijuana for more than just "experimentation."
  - Marijuana within the past three years or for a substantial period of time.[20]
- Problem Child backgrounds – These applicants have issues with their backgrounds that must be resolved or adjudicated before they move along to the next step. This could be as simple as failing to update Selective Service information or resolving unpaid traffic fines. Decisions are made on a case-by-case basis for persons that fall into this category.

---

[19] The Lautenberg Amendment - Individuals who have been convicted of a misdemeanor crime of domestic violence are ineligible to possess or receive firearms and therefore cannot be employed as federal law enforcement officer. A "crime of domestic violence" is defined as a misdemeanor under federal or State law which involves the use or attempted use of physical force, or the threatened use of a deadly weapon, by a current or former spouse, parent, or guardian of the victim, by a person with whom the victim shares a child in common, by a person who is cohabiting with or has cohabitated with the victim as a spouse, parent, or guardian, or by a person similarly situated to a spouse, parent, or guardian of the victim. A person will not be considered to have been convicted of a crime of domestic violence unless (1) the person was represented by a counsel in the case, or had knowingly and intelligently waived the right to counsel; and (2) if the person was entitled to a jury trial in the jurisdiction in which the case was to be tried, the person either received a jury trial or knowingly and intelligently waived the right to a jury trial by pleading guilty or otherwise. A person shall not be considered to have been convicted if the conviction has been set aside or expunged or is an offense for which the person has been pardoned or has had civil rights restored, unless the pardon, expungement, or restoration of civil rights expressly provided that the person may not ship, transport, possess, or receive firearms.

[20] http://www.usatoday.com/news/washington/2007-08-01-fbi_N.htm

Standard Form 86

The standard form (SF) 86 is normally used to gather information from the applicant for the background investigation. I suggest completing this form prior to seeking employment in federal law enforcement so you obtain an understanding of the background information agencies are concerned about. One of the creative ways some agencies have tried to reduce the length of time it takes to do a background investigation is by conducting the background investigation while the employee is going through basic training. As you can imagine, there can be some real negative consequences and embarrassment with this practice, i.e., arresting a trainee at the academy on an outstanding warrant for homicide does not make for good publicity. Expect that throughout your federal career, the SF 86 will be used to periodically update your security clearance. A portable document file of the SF 86 can be found at: http://www.opm.gov/forms/pdf_fill/SF86.pdf.

Baby Boomer Full-Time Equivalent Positions

Those in the human resources world of the federal government have a special name for a permanent job position. A permanent position is called a full-time equivalent or FTE. Most law enforcement positions are filled by FTE rather than term or temporary positions. The charts on the following pages visually show the FTE age distribution for most of the federal police work force. For those in the LEO chart, located to the left, there is a mandatory 57 years-of-age retirement policy. These are the officers covered under 6C or similar retirement systems. There is no choice in the matter; they must retire at age 57.

In comparison, the chart on the right is equally impressive; however, these non-6C law enforcement employees are not required to retire at a specific age. Note this chart is mislabeled by OPM as GS Age distribution rather it should indicate Non-LEO or Non-Covered. Keep in mind, in the government world of law enforcement jobs, it is a good business practice to fill an FTE quickly rather than leaving it open for a long time. It is possible, but not probable; the government will have a hiring freeze and try to downsize the workforce. Given the state of world affairs, I doubt any downsizing would last long in federal law enforcement. No matter how you look at it, the Feds will be hiring lots of people for many years to come. Check out the graphs, the baby boomers are retiring! Massive numbers of people will be required to replace them in the next few years.

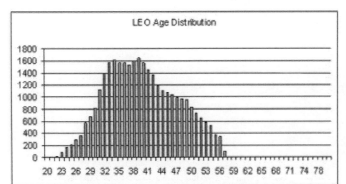
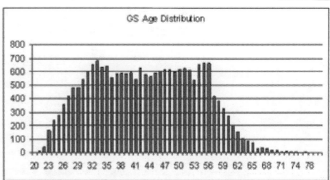

Category	Number	Mean
LEO	32,764	40.0
Non-LEO	20,992	43.0

The table and charts above present certain statistical characteristics of selected relevant employee groups with LEO (6C) retirement coverage and without LEO retirement coverage (non-covered). While the sample is quite large, it is not the entire universe of LEOs and non-LEOs. The table indicates that individuals in the LEO category have an average age of nearly 40 years, while individuals in the non-LEO category have an average age of nearly 43 years. Three-fourths (75.1 percent) of the LEO group is 45 or younger, while just over one-half (57.4 percent) of the non-LEO group is 45 or under.

Statistical Analysis of Combined Age Distribution

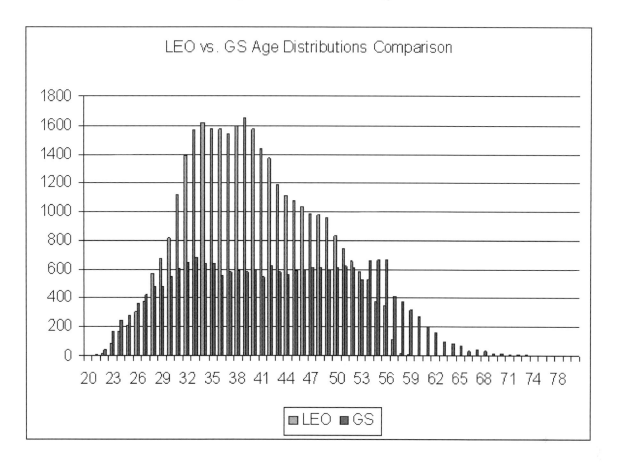

It is apparent the two groups have two distinctly different age distributions. The LEO (6C) group is more clustered around its average age, and the distribution indicates a younger population than the GS group. The GS (non-covered) group has a more even distribution of ages.

Difficulties in Getting Qualified Applicants

Unbelievably, it is difficult to get qualified applicants for federal law enforcement positions. There may be a number of systemic reasons why the federal government has a hard time recruiting and selecting law enforcement officers. First, there is the issue of advertising/marketing. Everyone has seen professional military recruiting ads for the Army, Navy, Air Force, and Marines. However, have you ever seen an advertisement for a federal law enforcement agency? Likely not and here is why.

There are two legal restrictions on agency public relations activities and propaganda. A law, 5 U.S.C. 3107, prohibits the use of appropriated funds to hire publicity experts. Secondly, appropriations law "publicity and propaganda" clauses restrict the use of funds for puffery of an agency, purely partisan communications, and covert propaganda.[21] Because of this, most federal law enforcement agencies do not market themselves well. The three main methods job seekers use to find out about federal positions are by word of mouth, through the Internet, or more recently by news stories on major policy changes such as Immigration reform. Even when an agency is able to advertise, they run into problems. For example: The National Football League refused to run a recruitment ad for the Border Patrol ...saying it was "controversial" because it mentioned duties such as fighting terrorism and stopping drugs and illegal aliens at the border.[22]

Certainly advertising is one issue but there are also other reasons for recruiting and selecting problems. The biggest problem that I hear about from new recruits is the length of time it takes from submitting a resume to actually entering on duty. This process can easily take a year or longer. For entry-level positions, potential applicants during this yearlong wait will likely be in another job while waiting for the Feds to make an offer. If they are successful in the other job, they may be moving up that other career ladder. The best and brightest potential applicants are then forced to choose between the proverbial "a bird in the hand versus the two in the bush." Other situations such as relationships or children could occur during this yearlong delay. Relationships and family responsibilities with children often deter potential applicants that are in a secure job from switching to a new job that requires successful completion of basic training and a probationary period.

The good news is that federal agencies are aware of the time factor problem and most agencies are actively trying to minimize the time it takes to fill a position. In fact, a Federal Protective Service Officer attending basic training in 2007 told me it only took him about four months to get through the entire process from applying to appointment. He and I were both surprised at how fast that occurred.

---

[21] http://www.fas.org/sgp/crs/RL32750.pdf
[22] http://washingtontimes.com/national/20070213-115739-3816r_page2.htm

With regard to how quickly you can enter on duty, the background suitability and security process is lengthy and there is no way around it. The bottom line is the background suitability and security process is a necessary vetting step that is not going away. The fact that an applicant already has a security clearance or has recently completed a background check may be just the positive attribute that differentiates one applicant from the others, particularly if the agency needs someone in the position quickly.

Pay and compensation is a third issue often cited by agencies regarding problems with recruiting. There are some very antiquated pay systems in existence. The General Schedule (GS) pay scale is a great example of one such archaic structure. However, from my standpoint, the only real inequities with the GS scale are for employees that live in major metropolitan areas. That information tells you a little about my biases; it would require a lot of money to get me to move to a city. Even with the locality pay adjustments, the low starting grades do not seem enough to attract the best and brightest to major cities. This is an advantage for a prospective employee that is willing to tough-it-out for a few years. If you are having trouble getting your foot in the door, I recommend that you use the laws of supply and demand in your favor and apply for locations where others will not go. Usually, that includes all of the major metropolitan areas but other areas that are hard to recruit job applicants include rural communities and some less desirable locations outside the continental United States.

Chapter 3: Finding the Agency and Job Right for You

When it comes to figuring out what federal law enforcement job is right for you, it really is like being a mosquito in a nudist colony. There are so many choices, where do you start? Well, let us start by understanding some of the major factors to consider within federal law enforcement employment.

Uniformed Officer

Special Agent

Inspections

Corrections

From my perspective, the most important factor to consider by a new applicant seeking a federal law enforcement career is the actual "law enforcement" status of the job. In the beginning of this guide, I stated, "all federal law enforcement jobs are not created equal." Here is where the inequality rears its ugly head. The following few sentences are worth repeating from Chapter 1.

A law enforcement job, for federal purposes, is not defined by whether the person in the position caries a gun and makes arrests. OPM's definition covering most new employees' states: A "law enforcement officer" is an employee whose primary duties are the "investigation, apprehension, and detention of individuals suspected or convicted of offenses against the criminal laws of the United States.[23] Under this definition, many federal police jobs are not classified as law enforcement for the purpose of retirement. The positions that meet the 6C definition of law enforcement have special advantages regarding minimum retirement age and retirement annuity (pension).

Congress has extended special retirement coverage to Park Police, Capitol Police, and Supreme Court Police. However, their standard police work of maintaining law and order, protecting life and property falls outside the definition of "law enforcement officer" for retirement purposes. Their duties are not primarily the "investigation, apprehension, or detention of individuals suspected or convicted of offenses against the criminal laws of the United States." While Park Police Officers, Capitol Police Officers, and Supreme Court Police officers receive enhanced retirement benefits similarly situated federal police officers, such as police officers at the Department of Defense, the Department of Veterans Affairs, the Mint, the Bureau of Engraving and Printing, and many officers in the Department of Homeland Security, are not entitled to the same treatment.

People in their twenties typically do not have the long term strategic thinking to value the importance of a specialized retirement package. Consider this: If there were one thing I could do over with regard to my career choices, it would be to ensure that I was in a law enforcement retirement position as early as possible. The law enforcement retirement issue may not be as important for those that plan to work past the age of 57. A better alternative for people that want to work past age 57 would be to retire from a 6C job and then find a non-covered police job, i.e., reemployed annuitant, or civilian background investigator. For more detailed information on retirement, refer to Chapter 5. It is worth noting that OPM clearly recognizes the disparity between non-law enforcement police jobs and law enforcement jobs with regard to retirement systems and the problems it creates with recruiting and retention. However, due to prohibitive costs, it is unlikely OPM's recommendations to Congress to remedy the inequity within law enforcement and non-law enforcement police retirements will occur. My advice, get into a 6C covered position as soon as possible.

---

[23] http://www2.opm.gov/oca/leo_report04/part_ii.asp#b

Competitive versus Excepted Service

The competitive or Excepted Service categorization of a position you seek is an important considerations when deciding which agencies and jobs are right for you. It is technically more correct to think of excepted and Competitive Service as occurring at various levels such as government Branches, Departments, Agencies, Positions, and under certain hiring authorities. However, let us keep things simple by having a representative list of excepted and Competitive Service job positions (see the following page).

The one caveat to this partial listing of federal law enforcement job positions is that many if not all agencies are taking advantage of hiring authorities which will temporarily hold new employees in the Excepted Service category. Under these special hiring authorities, the government has allowed extraordinary methods to hire someone without going through the "normal" competitive process. As you look throughout the list, you will quickly discover there are far more federal police positions in the Competitive Service than the Excepted Service.

So what is the big deal? Why is the class of job (competitive vs. excepted) significant for someone applying for a law enforcement job? I will answer that by stating: There are two important reasons you should desire a Competitive Service position rather than an Excepted Service position. Firstly, it is considerably more difficult for the employing agency to fire a Competitive Service employee in comparison to the process used to fire an Excepted Service employee. The Competitive Service has built-in protections. Specifically, there are employee appeal rights for adverse actions such as being fired. There is some controversy around this issue. Cynics view the government's use of the Excepted Service as merely a tactic to get around employee rights. With regard to recommendations on this issue, opinions vary, some say "… steer clear of Excepted Service positions unless you are confident that you can leave government at any given moment."[24] When I asked officers that worked in the Excepted Service, I could get no examples of situations where employees were fired arbitrarily. However, the firing of a dozen United States Attorneys by the Department of Justice in 2007 provides a glimpse of what could happen to any Excepted Service employee.

---

[24]
http://community.federalsoup.com/4/OpenTopic?a=tpc&s=4944011921&f=2024011031&m=8101095731

Department	Agency	Position	Excepted	Competitive
Agriculture	Forest Service	Criminal Investigator		X
Agriculture	Forest Service	Uniformed Law Enforcement Officer		X
Air Force	Air Force Personnel Center	Security Guard		X
Air Force	Office of Special Investigations	Criminal Investigator		X
Army	Army Chemical Materials Agency	Security Guard		X
Army	Army Communications Electronics Command	Police Officer		X
Army	Army Installation Management Agency	Police Officer		X
Army	Army Installation Management Agency	Detective		X
Army	Army Medical Command	Police Officer		X
Commerce	Bureau of Industry and Security	Criminal Investigator		X
Commerce	National Marine Fisheries	Criminal Investigator		X
Defense	Armed Forces Retirement Homes	Security Guard		X
Defense	Defense Criminal Investigative Service	Criminal Investigator		X
Defense	Defense Intelligence Agency	Security Officer		X
Defense	Pentagon Force Protection	Police Officer		X
Energy	Department of Energy	Criminal Investigator		X
Energy	Office of Secure Transportation	Nuclear Material Couriers		X
Health & Human Sen	Food and Drug Administration	Criminal Investigator		X
Health and Human S	Health & Human Services	Security Guard		X
Homeland Security	Coast Guard	Criminal Investigator		X
Homeland Security	Customs and Border Protection	Border Patrol Agent		X
Homeland Security	Customs and Border Protection	Officer (formerly Inspector)		X
Homeland Security	Customs and Border Protection	Technical Enforcement Officer		X
Homeland Security	Customs and Border Protection	Investigative Program Specialist (Polygraph Examiner)		X
Homeland Security	Customs and Border Protection	Marine Officer		X
Homeland Security	Customs and Border Protection	Air Interdiction Agents (Pilot)		X
Homeland Security	Customs and Border Protection	Federal Protective Service Police Officer		X
Homeland Security	Customs and Border Protection	Federal Protective Service Investigator		X
Homeland Security	Customs and Border Protection	Import Specialist		X
Homeland Security	Federal Law Enforcement Training Center	Instructor		X
Homeland Security	Federal Law Enforcement Training Center	Law Enforcement Program Specialist		X
Homeland Security	Immigration and Customs Enforcement	Criminal Investigator		X
Homeland Security	Immigration and Customs Enforcement	Detention and Deportation Officer		X
Homeland Security	Immigration and Customs Enforcement	Investigative Assistant		X
Homeland Security	Immigration and Customs Enforcement	Deportation Officer		X
Homeland Security	Immigration and Customs Enforcement	Physical Security Specialist		X
Homeland Security	Transportation Security Agency	Federal Air Marshal	X	
Homeland Security	Transportation Security Agency	Transportation Security Officer (Screener)	X	
Homeland Security	Transportation Security Agency	Transportation Security Specialist	X	
Independent	Central Intelligence Agency	Security Protective Officer	X	
Independent	Environmental Protection Agency	Criminal Investigator		X
Independent	Office of Personnel Management	Background Investigator		X
Independent	Office of Personnel Management	Criminal Investigator		X
Independent	Postal Service	Criminal Investigator		X
Interior	Bureau of Indian Affairs	Criminal Investigator		X
Interior	Bureau of Land Management	Park Ranger (Law Enforcement or Protection)		X
Interior	Fish And Wildlife Service	Criminal Investigator		X
Interior	Fish And Wildlife Service	Park Ranger (Law Enforcement/Refuge)		X
Interior	National Park Service	Park Police Officer		X
Interior	National Park Service	Park Ranger (Law Enforcement or Protection)		X
Interior	National Park Service	Criminal Investigator		X
Justice	Bureau of Alcohol, Tobacco and Firearms	Criminal Investigator		X
Justice	Bureau of Prisons	Correctional Officer		X
Justice	Drug Enforcement Agency	Criminal Investigator		X
Justice	Drug Enforcement Agency	Diversion Investigator		X
Justice	Drug Enforcement Agency	Criminal Investigator		X
Justice	Federal Bureau of Investigations	Criminal Investigator	X	
Justice	Federal Bureau of Investigations	Uniformed Officer	X	
Justice	Marshals	Criminal Investigative Deputy Marshal		X
Justice	Marshals	Deputy Marshal		X
Justice	Marshals	Detention Enforcement Officer		X
Justice	Office of the Inspector General	Criminal Investigator		X
Navy	Naval Criminal Investigative Service	Criminal Investigator		X
Navy	Navy	Physical Security Specialist		X
Navy	US Marine Corps	Police Officer		X
State	Diplomatic Security	Criminal Investigator	X	
Treasury	Bureau of Engraving and Printing	Police Officer		X
Treasury	Internal Revenue Service	Criminal Investigator		X
Treasury	Mint	Police Officer		X
Treasury	Secret Service	Uniformed Officer		X
Treasury	Secret Service	Criminal Investigator		X
Treasury	Secret Service	Protective Support Assistant (OA)		X
Veterans Affairs	Inspector General	Criminal Investigator		X
Independent	Supreme Court	Police Officer	X	
Independent	Capitol Police	Police Officer	X	
Independent	Government Printing Office	Police Officer		X
Independent	Library of Congress	Police Officer	X	

The second and more important reason to seek a Competitive Service position is to gain career or career conditional status so you can apply for Merit Promotion Vacancy Announcements. Career and career conditional status is also known as competitive status. Competitive status is one of the requirements for applicants under Merit Promotion Vacancy Announcements. Excepted Service employees generally do not gain competitive status and miss the opportunities to apply for a great many jobs.

Competitive status is an employee's basic eligibility for noncompetitive assignment (e.g., by transfer, promotion, reassignment, demotion, or reinstatement) to a position in the Competitive Service without having to compete with members of the public in an open competitive examination. Competitive status belongs to an employee, not to a position. A person on a career or career conditional appointment acquires competitive status upon satisfactory completion of a probationary period. It may also be granted by statute, Executive Order, or the civil service rules without competitive examination, for example; former overseas employees.[25] For more information about exceptions to the competitive status rules go to http://www.opm.gov/employ/html/sroa2.asp.

My advice, if you decide that you want to work as a Capitol Police Officer or an FBI Special Agent, don't let the Excepted Service job class dissuade you from applying for those positions. These are two great agencies. However, given the choice between two agencies, one in the Competitive Service and the other in the Excepted Service, I would take the Competitive Service job. For example, you are pursuing opportunities with the FBI and the Secret Service as a Special Agent, everything else being equal, go for the Secret Service job because it is in the Competitive Service. Remember my caveat, under certain hiring authorities like internships you will automatically begin in the Excepted Service when in fact the position may normally be in the Competitive Service.

The reality is that many coworkers I spoke to regarding this issue did not even realize there were differences in the two systems. As a law enforcement supervisor, I wish I could work in the Excepted Service because it would make my life easier when dealing with poor performers; however, as an employee I like my Competitive Service protections. It may be a moot point in the long term because the trend for the federal government is to move away from industrial age based human resource systems. For more information on the competitive and Excepted Service go to: http://www.USAJobs.gov/EI6.asp.

---

[25] http://www.doi.gov/hrm/pmanager/st6a.html

Agency (Corporate) Culture

How your personality fits in with an agency's culture is a third major factor to consider regarding which agency and job is right for you. An agency's culture can be defined as the personality of the organization. It guides how employees think, act, and feel. It is in essence the character of the agency and includes elements like core values, ethics, and rules of behavior. Agency culture can be expressed in such things as a mission statement, web pages, press reports, enforcement actions, or even in the building style and decorations within office areas. It even trickles down to the badges, credentials, uniforms, types of weapons carried, formality used in conversations, amount of overtime expected, and employee job titles.

While agency culture to some may sound esoteric and a little on the touchy-feely side, there is nothing worse for all concerned parties than a complete mismatch between an employee and employer. The bottom line is that you will likely do well in an organization that has a similar mindset with regard to your expectations of police work. Conversely, you will likely do poorly with an agency that has vastly different expectations of your police work. For example, if you see yourself as a hard charging, get your hands dirty, door kicking, thug arresting street cop; you may want to gravitate towards DEA and ATF. On the other hand, if you enjoy accounting and indoor office paperwork you should pursue Inspector General Special Agent positions.

I think you can get a good feel about agency culture through agency Web site information, news articles, and by talking to recruiters. The reality is that you will never really know the culture until you have worked many months for an agency, but you can get the big picture through research and observation. It is also important to note that agency culture is likely to vary from one office to another and does typically change slowly over time. [26]

At the risk of offending some of my friends, I will try to define some broad categories within the federal law enforcement community by using stereotypes. The difficulty in defining a job stereotype is that traits and characteristics of the stereotype will not hold true for everyone within the group and often times the stereotype does not even apply to a majority. That being said, here is my best attempt. As a whole, federal officers are conservative in nature and are more likely to align themselves with the tenants of the Republican Party rather than the political ideology of the Democrats. Officers are typically raised in middle to lower-middle class families and usually share the values of rural America. Whether by upbringing or as a causal effect of law enforcement work, most federal officers have a conservative political viewpoint. Commonly, a close friend or relative has worked in law enforcement.

---

[26]http://www.quintcareers.com/employer_corporate_culture.html

Within the federal law enforcement occupations, I have recognized four distinct sub-job categories.

- Special Agents
- Uniformed Officers
- Inspections
- Corrections

Special Agents

Special Agents (Criminal Investigators or CIs, 1811s) can be categorized as the white-collar workforce for the Feds. Special Agents usually have a four-year college degree and are more casual than their uniformed brothers and sisters. They are in good physical condition. Two sports that may typify the 1811 persona are soccer and golf. These officers are generally more liberal than other federal officers and are not shy about asking the question "Why?" Special Agents are likely to have graduated from college with a Bachelor's degree in Criminal Justice or Accounting and many have started or completed their Master's degree. Job satisfaction is more important than the paycheck.

Uniformed Officers

In contrast, uniformed officers typically have a military background or demeanor and are the blue-collar arm of the federal police workforce. Their personality is more of a follower, they are more regimented and compliance oriented than the CIs. Basketball would be a sport that describes their identity. Those that have an undergraduate degree are likely to have matriculated in a non-traditional manner, i.e. night school, online, and not immediately following high school. The pay for these employees is slightly more important than the quality of the work conditions.

Inspections

Inspectional officers, such as CBP Officers working at a border Port of Entry, are a mixed bag. This eclectic group has a combination of traits and personalities from the first two categories. Officers that enter into this career later in life are more like the uniformed officers while the younger inspectional officers are more like the Special Agents. CBP Officers are expected to receive 6C coverage in the near future. Their 6C coverage was approved by law but not funded. It will be interesting to see how the 6C change affects their long-term retention of criminal investigative types. I predict their whole persona will change and only old timers like me will remember them as Inspectors. The name change from Customs Inspectors to CBP Officers has already paid dividends in a more positive law enforcement image.

Corrections

Correctional officers typically come from a rural background and have a high school degree although many have had some college course work. Football or wrestling are their descriptive sports. The paycheck and health benefits are their main reason for the job. They are likely to have started a family very young in their life and they work hard and play hard.

Top Job Picks

Listed below are a number of my top law enforcement job picks in alphabetical order by agency. If you do not see a job listed, do not assume it is a bad one. In some cases, I have provided my opinion regarding the agency culture and the quality of the organization in relation to the others. In some cases, the opinion was provided from an official OPM report. Remember the adage that "beauty is in the eye of the beholder" so you understand that my observations are certainly biased by my personal likes and dislikes.

Air Force Office of Special Investigations (OSI)

The Air Force OSI has been the Air Force's major investigative service since 1948. The agency reports to the Inspector General, Office of the Secretary of the Air Force. OSI consists of more than 2900 federal agents and support personnel.[27] OSI provides professional investigative services to commanders of all Air Force activities. Its primary responsibilities are criminal investigations and counterintelligence services. The command focuses on four priorities:

- Detect and provide early warning of worldwide threats to the Air Force;
- Identify and resolve crime impacting Air Force readiness or good order and discipline;
- Combat threats to Air Force information systems and technologies; and
- Defeat and deter fraud in the acquisition of Air Force prioritized weapons systems.

Like the Coast Guard and Army, the Air Force OSI has positions for enlisted personnel, officers, and civilians. In addition to regularly announced vacancies, the Air Force Personnel Center offers OSI Special Agent positions through its PALACE ACQUIRE Program, which hires approximately 10 new agents per year. The PALACE Acquire Intern Program targets college graduates for a two to three year training and development program. To qualify, a minimum undergraduate cumulative grade point average of 3.45 on a 4.0 scale is required, or the graduate must rank in the top 10 percent of his or her undergraduate class overall, or in a major subdivision, e.g., School of Business.[28]

---

[27] http://www.osi.andrews.af.mil/
[28] http://www.jobweb.com/employer/matrix/airforce.htm

Two separate types of Special Agent positions exist within this program: those that require foreign language fluency and those that do not. For each type, one window of opportunity exists per year to apply, usually in June. Interested applicants must request an application package while the window is open. To learn more about when and how to apply, visit Air Force Personnel Center. There, you will also find information about the positions, qualifications, and career advancement.

Army Criminal Investigative Division (CID)

The mission of CID is to investigate and deter serious crimes in which the Army has an interest. CID collects, analyzes processes and disseminates criminal intelligence; conducts protective service operations; provides forensic laboratory support to all Department of Defense investigative agencies, and maintains Army criminal records. CID also provides criminal investigative support to all Army elements and deploys on short notice in support of contingency operations worldwide. CID is organized in a similar manner as the Coast Guard in that Special Agents can come from enlisted ranks, the Reserves, or Civilian personnel.

CID is a worldwide command with fewer than 2000 Soldiers and civilians and approximately 900 Special Agents. CID Special Agents primarily investigate felony level crime across the Army and provide investigative support to field commanders. They conduct a wide variety of investigations to include deaths, sexual assault, armed robbery, procurement fraud, computer crimes, counter-drug operations and war crimes. CID agents also provide counter-terrorism support, criminal intelligence support, force protection, forensic laboratory investigative support, and protective services for key Department of Defense and senior Army leadership.

CID supports the Army in peacetime and in war. CID maintains its primary investigative responsibilities while also conducting contingency operations and battlefield missions. These missions include logistics security, criminal intelligence, criminal investigations that may include war crimes, anti-terrorism support, protective service operations and force protection operations. Force protection operations help safeguard soldiers, civilian employees, family members, and facilities and equipment in a combat or expeditionary environment. Performing these missions during conflict or operations other than war requires the same skills CID investigators use daily in support of commanders during peacetime. During war, investigations can also focus on sabotage, diversion of supplies and equipment and profiteering to ensure that all equipment and supplies intended for Soldiers actually reach them.[29] For information on available positions, please check the civilian personnel online Web site.[30]

---

[29] http://www.cid.army.mil/faqs.htm#relatedforms
[30] http://www.cid.army.mil/recruiting.htm

Bureau of Alcohol, Tobacco, Firearms, and Explosives (BATF)

BATF agents regulate and investigate violations of federal firearms and explosives laws, as well as federal alcohol and tobacco tax regulations.[31] Although a dissimilar mission, BATF shares the same high quality reputation with the Marshals Service and both are now under the Department of Justice. This is an excellent agency to work with. Applicants for Special Agent jobs with the BATF must have a bachelor's degree, a minimum of three years' related work experience, or a combination of education and experience. Under current recruitment efforts, all applicants are required to take and pass an ATF sponsored Treasury Enforcement Agent exam. Test results will be valid for a period of three years from the date of the exam. For hiring/testing updates, please contact the ATF Recruitment and Hiring Center periodically at 202-648-9100.

BATF will only consider a lateral announcement when the need arises. Under current recruitment efforts, current 1811's are welcome to apply however; they will only be considered at the GS 5, GS 7, or GS 9 grade level. They will also be required to leave the Competitive Service and enter the Excepted Service for a period of three years.[32] Prospective Special Agents undergo 11 weeks of initial criminal investigation training at the Federal Law Enforcement Training Center in Glynco, Georgia, and another 17 weeks of specialized training. BATF has an excellent reputation as an agency that confronts some of the most violent criminals. As an agency, they have undergone periods of time when they looked like they would be dismantled and their mission swallowed up by other federal entities. This type of drastic change is unlikely to occur in the near future but long timers have seen this pendulum swing back and forth over time.

Coast Guard Investigative Service (CGIS)

As the fourth branch of the military that operates under the Department of Homeland Security during peacetime, the Coast Guard is an excellent agency for a law enforcement career. Although many positions within the Coast Guard perform law enforcement functions, the focus of this text is on criminal investigative positions within the Coast Guard Investigative Service (CGIS). The CGIS is a federal investigative and protective program established to carry out the Coast Guard's internal and external criminal investigations; to assist in providing personal security services; to protect the welfare of Coast Guard people; to aid in preserving the internal integrity of the Coast Guard; and to support Coast Guard missions worldwide. The CGIS is a centralized directorship managed by a professional criminal investigator who reports to the Assistant Commandant for Intelligence.

---

[31] http://www.opm.gov/oca/wage/index.asp
[32] http://www.atf.treas.gov/jobs/sa_faq.htm

The CGIS functions outside the Coast Guard's operational chain of command. CGIS is primarily made up of three groups of individuals:

- USCG Active Duty Chief Warrant Officers (CWO) and Petty Officers. These individuals are of different specialties and ratings and rotate into CGIS for a tour of duty or consecutive tours of duty. These individuals have served in the Coast Guard and are selected for CGIS on a "best qualified" basis. CWO positions are normally filled by enlisted Special Agents appointed to CWO. Enlisted personnel must be E-6 and above to apply. Each summer, CGIS solicits for applicants to fill enlisted active duty positions.
- USCG Reserve Personnel. These personnel are Chief Warrant Officers (Investigators) and Petty Officers serving in the Reserve Investigator Rating (IV). Personnel interested in joining the Coast Guard Reserve should visit the CG Reserve Web Page for more information.
- Full-time civilian - GS 1811 Special Agents. These personnel are hired from qualified civilian applicants. Generally, law enforcement experience is required to be hired by CGIS. Newly hired Special Agents receive additional law enforcement training as necessary and are eligible for assignment throughout the United States and its territories. Job openings are based on the needs of the service and follow regular government hiring practices. The job openings are announced under the title, "Criminal Investigator" on the Coast Guard Personnel Command Web site http://www.uscg.mil/hq/cgpc/cpm/jobs/vacancy.htm and USAJobs.

Customs and Border Protection (CBP)

CBP employees prevent terrorists and terrorist weapons from entering the United States while facilitating the flow of legitimate trade and travel. CBP and Immigration and Customs Enforcement are similar organizations in they were both formed in part from the Immigration and Naturalization Service and the Customs Service, neither of which exist any longer. The main difference between ICE and CBP is that ICE performs mainly investigative, physical security and deportation functions while CBP provides inspection and patrol functions enforcing Customs and Immigration Laws. One of the issues for current and future employees of CBP is the overall morale of their employees. With the forced integration of the agencies to form CBP there have been some real growing pains. The morale issue represents an opportunity for applicants, as there may be a higher turnover rate within CBP as people leave for other agencies. There are many law enforcement positions within CBP worth pursuing.

- Air Enforcement Officer
- CBP Officers
- Border Patrol Agents
- Marine Interdiction Agents

Air Enforcement Officers – These are the pilots of aircraft and unmanned aircraft systems. They operate a fleet of 258 aircraft, including UH-60 Black Hawk helicopters, Astar helicopters, as well as C-210, C-12, and long-range P-3 Orion fixed-wing aircraft.

The P-3s conduct air detection and monitoring missions in drug source and transit zones, including South and Central America, the Eastern Pacific, and the Caribbean, under the aegis of the Joint Inter-agency Task Force-South, a unit of the United States Southern Command, as well as domestic air security and crisis response missions. They patrol the skies to prevent the illegal entry of weapons of terror, while interdicting illegal narcotics and preventing the illegal entry of undocumented aliens. They fly some of the most sophisticated aircraft in some of the most demanding situations and environments. Air Enforcement Officers conduct covert and overt operations against terrorist activities.[33]

Border Patrol Agents – These mobile uniformed officers work between the Ports of Entry covered by CBP Officers. The Border Patrol has a strong *esprit de corps* and great law enforcement reputation. Their primary mission is the protection of our borders by detecting and preventing the smuggling and unlawful entry of undocumented aliens into the United States and to apprehend those persons found in the United States in violation of the Immigration laws. With the increase in drug smuggling operations, one of Border Patrol's primary duties is drug interdiction along the land borders, between all the United States land Ports of Entry.[34] Initial appointments are usually to the Southern Border, e.g., Texas, New Mexico, California.

CBP Officers – These uniformed officers work at one of the 300 plus Ports of Entry throughout the country and at various international locations. The Ports of Entry include airports, seaports and land borders and new employees could be hired for anyone of these locations. The Officer's primary responsibility is to detect and prevent terrorists and weapons of mass destruction from entering the United States, while facilitating the orderly flow of legitimate trade and travelers. This requires enforcing laws related to revenue and trade, seizure of contraband, interdiction of agricultural pests and diseases, and admissibility of persons.

CBP Officers perform the full range of inspection, passenger and cargo analysis, examination and law enforcement activities relating to the arrival and departure of persons, merchandise and conveyances such as cars, trucks, aircraft, and ships at the Ports of Entry. CBP Officers also have a special group of K-9 dog handlers formerly known as Canine Enforcement Officers. They use specially trained detector dogs to interdict large quantities of illegal narcotic substances, smuggled agriculture products, and unreported currency at our nation's Ports of Entry. The Canine Enforcement Program is also involved in specialized detection programs aimed at combating terrorist threats at our nation's borders and international airports.

Marine Interdiction Agents (MIAs) – MIAs are the boat operators that work with the air interdiction operators to patrol the vast waterways around the United States and its territories. CBP MIAs operate 70 different types of marine vessels and procures, outfits, and trains operators for a fleet totaling over 200 vessels. Additionally, this fleet includes 39-foot interceptor vessels, 33-foot SAFE boats, various coastal enforcement craft, and larger oceangoing support and radar platform vessels. The CBP vessels operate mostly

---

[33]http://cbp.gov/xp/cgov/careers/customs_careers/air_marine/cbp_pilot_lp.xml
[34] http://cbp.gov/xp/cgov/careers/customs_careers/border_careers/bp_agent/working_for_bp.xml

along northern and southern United States maritime borders and in United States seaports. MIA crews work closely to coordinate efforts with the Coast Guard, Navy, and other state and local law enforcement organizations.[35]

Diplomatic Security

The Department of State, Bureau of Diplomatic Security (DS) Special Agents are engaged in the battle against terrorism. Overseas, they advise ambassadors on all security matters and manage a complex range of security programs designed to protect personnel, facilities, and information. In the United States, they investigate passport and visa fraud, conduct personnel security investigations, issue security clearances, and protect the Secretary of State and a number of foreign dignitaries. They also train foreign civilian police and administer a counter-terrorism reward program.[36] This agency has some great training and many travel opportunities; however, if you have your heart set on living in America this job is not for you. It is likely that at some point in a career as a DS Special Agent you will work oversees in a third world country. That novelty can wear off fast.

Drug Enforcement Administration (DEA)

DEA Special Agents enforce laws and regulations relating to illegal drugs. Not only is the DEA the lead agency for domestic enforcement of federal drug laws, it also has sole responsibility for coordinating and pursuing United States drug investigations abroad. Agents may conduct complex criminal investigations, carry out surveillance of criminals, and infiltrate illicit drug organizations using undercover techniques.[37]

Working undercover as a DEA Special Agent takes a special kind of person and as you would expect those working conditions can be very stressful to family and other relationships. DEA Special Agents have a great reputation with their criminal investigative peers. Applicants for Special Agent jobs with the DEA must have a college degree with at least a 2.95 grade point average or specialized skills or work experience, such as foreign language fluency, technical skills, law enforcement experience, or accounting experience. DEA Special Agents undergo 14 weeks of specialized training at the FBI Academy in Quantico, Virginia.

Federal Bureau of Investigation (FBI)

The FBI has two separate and distinct law enforcement entities: Special Agents and Police Officers. FBI Special Agents are the Government's principal investigators responsible for investigating violations of more than 200 categories of federal law and conducting sensitive national security investigations. Special Agents may conduct surveillance, monitor court authorized wiretaps, examine business records, investigate white-collar crime, or participate in sensitive undercover assignments. The FBI

---

[35]http://cbp.gov/xp/cgov/careers/customs_careers/air_marine/cbp_pilot_lp.xml
[36] http://www.opm.gov/oca/wage/index.asp
[37] http://www.opm.gov/oca/wage/index.asp

investigates organized crime, public corruption, financial crime, and fraud against the government, bribery, copyright infringement, civil rights violations, bank robbery, extortion, kidnapping, air piracy, terrorism, espionage, interstate criminal activity, drug trafficking, and other violations of federal statutes. [38] Since the days of J. Edgar Hoover, the FBI has been known for having a professional law enforcement organization. Expect strict dress codes and rules of conduct, although, this is more relaxed than years past.

The FBI Special Agents have a reputation of doing a great job but also are not shy about taking credit for doing a great job. To be considered for appointment as an FBI agent, an applicant must be a graduate of an accredited law school or a college graduate with one of the following: a major in accounting, electrical engineering, or information technology; fluency in a foreign language; or three years of related full-time work experience. All new agents undergo 18 weeks of training at the FBI Academy on the Marine Corps base in Quantico, Virginia.[39] The mission and culture of this organization should make the FBI Special Agent position one of the top choices for anyone seeking a criminal investigator position.

FBI Police Officers are the uniformed side of the house that provide protective security for FBI personnel and facilities and perform law enforcement duties at and around FBI facilities. FBI Police Officers are stationed in Washington, D.C. (FBI Headquarters and the Washington Field Office); Quantico, VA (FBI Academy, FBI Laboratory); New York City (New York Field Office); and Clarksburg, WV (FBI Criminal Justice Information Services Division).[40] If becoming an FBI Special Agent were your dream job, I would not recommend working as a FBI Police Officer. It is the exception rather than the rule for a uniformed FBI officer to become an FBI Special Agent through career advancement.

---

[38] http://www.opm.gov/oca/wage/index.asp
[39] http://www.opm.gov/oca/wage/index.asp
[40] http://www.fbijobs.gov/126.asp

Naval Criminal Investigative Service (NCIS)

NCIS is a worldwide federal law enforcement organization whose mission is to protect and serve the Navy and Marine Corps and their families. NCIS has approximately 1800 employees, 1100 of whom are civilian Special Agents, located in over 150 locations around the globe, including some aboard ships and carriers. NCIS grew out of Office of Naval Intelligence during World War I and its organization and mission has changed since that time. Presently, it is headed by a career law enforcement senior executive.[41] Many people are familiar with NCIS because of the hit TV series with the same abbreviation. NCIS Special Agents work criminal cases such as rapes and murders, which occur in their jurisdiction. With the Navy and Marine involvement in Iraq, the Special Agents are also involved with the interrogation of prisoners and interviewing informants. This agency is an excellent organization but competition for the jobs may be disproportionately high due to the hype from the TV series. NCIS has a thorough online informational package on the application process for becoming a Special Agent.

Federal Law Enforcement Training Center (FLETC)

FLETC is a training institution that develops the skills, knowledge, and professionalism of law enforcement officers from 80+ federal agencies in a unique inter-agency training organization. FLETC only has a few operational law enforcement officers in its security division although they do hire many law enforcement people that give up their badge and gun to become Instructors and Program Specialists. Generally, persons coming from a 6C position can continue their retirement coverage if they leave their federal agency and come to FLETC without a break in service as a Law Enforcement Instructor (secondary 6C coverage). FLETC hires Law Enforcement Instructors to teach a variety of courses and specialty areas. This listing provides a general idea of the types of material taught.

- Behavioral Sciences: Effective techniques of interviewing witnesses, victims, and suspects; recognizing stress sources and employing appropriate coping mechanisms to deal with stress.
- Computer & Financial Investigations: Detection and combating computer crimes and crimes where the computer is used by criminals to further illegal enterprises.
- Counter Terrorism: Anti-terrorism, physical security, officer safety and survival.
- Driver Training: Basic and advanced vehicle dynamics involving highway response, skid control, and defensive and offensive driving techniques.
- Enforcement Operations: Working with informants, conducting surveillance, executing search warrants, working undercover operations, radio communications, note taking and report writing, operational and patrol skills.
- Firearms: Use of revolvers, semi-automatic pistols and shoulder weapons utilizing safe handling, proficient employment and justifiable use of weapons.
- Forensics and Investigative Technologies: Techniques in fingerprinting, description and identification of persons, law enforcement photography, collection

---

[41] http://www.ncis.navy.mil/downloads/NCIS_Special_Agent_Applicant_Infobooklet.doc

and preservation of physical evidence, narcotics identification, rape investigation, and intelligence recognition.

- Legal: Fundamentals of the Constitution and the Bill of Rights as they relate to investigations, detention, arrest, searches, and seizures.
- Marine Training: Marine law enforcement operations, water navigation rules of the road, mechanical trouble shooting, pursuit, intercept, boarding and searching, and the use of weapons on a boat.
- Physical Techniques: Arrest techniques, self-defense, emergency medical procedures, water survival, physical conditioning. [42]

FLETC is noted for its family friendly attitude and most employees that switch agencies to join FLETC do so for quality of life reasons. Less overtime, night, weekend and shift work means more time with the family. Giving up the badge and gun is hardest part for most who make the switch.

Fish and Wildlife Service (FWS)

The Fish & Wildlife Service, an agency within the Department of Interior, is dedicated to conserving, protecting, and enhancing fish and wildlife and plants and their habitats for the continuing benefit of the American people. The top reasons why people choose to work for this agency are the job locations and work environment. From the Arctic Ocean to the South Pacific, from the Atlantic to the Caribbean, FWS personnel work to ensure that future generations of Americans will be able to enjoy nature's beauty and bounty and plays a pivotal role in safeguarding some of this nation's rich natural resources. There are three main positions that are of interest to law enforcement professionals.

1. Special Agents - are trained criminal investigators who enforce wildlife laws throughout the United States. They conduct investigations, which may include activities such as surveillance, undercover work, seizing contraband, making arrests, and preparing cases for court. They often work with other law enforcement authorities. They also are involved in public education and assistance.
2. Wildlife Inspectors - are the Nation's front-line defense against the illegal wildlife trade. Wildlife Inspectors are stationed at the Nation's major international airports, ocean ports, and border crossings. They stop illegal shipments, intercept smuggled wildlife and wildlife products such as animal skins, and help the United States fulfill its commitment to global wildlife conservation.
3. Refuge Officers – are law enforcement officers that protect wildlife from poaching and ensure the safety of visitors to the national wildlife refuges.[43]

Forest Service

The Forest Service is a bureau within the Department of Agriculture. As custodian of the National Forests and Grasslands, the Forest Service manages ecosystems on 191 million

---

[42] http://www.fletc.gov/employment/general-descriptions-of-instructor-positions
[43] http://www.fws.gov/hr/hr/employment.htm

acres of the Nation's lands. Resources on these lands are diverse, including range, timber, minerals, watersheds, wilderness, fish, and wildlife, each with cultural, scientific, recreational, or natural scenic values. Forest Service law enforcement personnel work outdoors in an interesting and exciting environment. The Forest Service protects lands and resources within its jurisdiction from wildfires, diseases, and forest insects, and from unfortunate instances of theft and vandalism. Law enforcement is essential to the management, use, and protection of National Forest lands and associated resources.

The Forest Service currently employs over 800 law enforcement personnel nationwide. With the rising number of visitors to the National Forests and Grasslands, the need for law enforcement personnel continues to grow. There are two main law enforcement positions within the Forest Service; they are Special Agents and Uniformed Law Enforcement Officers. Law enforcement positions are normally advertised and filled by the Special Agent in Charge (SAC) in the region with the vacancy. The Forest Service has offices throughout the United States and in Puerto Rico.

Special Agents plan and conduct investigations concerning possible violations of criminal and administrative provisions of the Forest Service and other statutes under the United States Code. Special Agent positions are located throughout the Nation, primarily in rural areas. Generally, only one Special Agent is assigned to an office.

Uniformed Law Enforcement Officers of the Forest Service enforce federal laws and regulations governing National Forest lands and resources. They establish a regular and recurring presence on vast amounts of public land, roads, and campgrounds, taking appropriate action when illegal activity is observed. In addition, Uniformed Officers assist Special Agents in executing search warrants.

Immigration and Customs Enforcement (ICE)

As the largest investigative arm of the Department of Homeland Security, ICE is primarily a law enforcement agency. The mission of ICE is to protect America and uphold public safety by targeting the people, money and materials that support terrorist and criminal activities. ICE enforces the nation's Customs and Immigration laws and provides security for federal buildings. Their enforcement mission is carried out by a wide variety of law enforcement, security and intelligence professionals, all of whom have the opportunity to make a personal contribution to the safety and security of our country.

ICE recruits two ways:

1. Special Agents are recruited by Special Agent recruiters with each of ICE's Special Agent in Charge (SAC) Office.
2. All other ICE positions are listed on USA Jobs, the main government jobs site. ICE is currently recruiting for entry-level Special Agents in limited numbers, only through direct contact with Special Agent recruiters located with each of ICE's SAC Offices. These vacancies are not posted on OPM's (OPM) USA Jobs Web site. If you are interested in becoming an ICE Special Agent, contact the nearest SAC Office and ask for the "Special Agent Recruiter." If you meet the basic qualifications and if ICE is actively recruiting Special Agents, the recruiter will advise you of the next steps in the application process.

Other ICE law enforcement occupations are comprised of a combination of both uniformed and non-uniformed law enforcement occupations, as well as a large number of administrative, technical, management, and mission support positions. As vacancies occur, with the exception of Special Agents, they are advertised on USAJobs, complete with position description, duties, requirements, and application procedures.

One component of ICE is the Federal Protective Service (FPS). FPS joined the Department of Homeland Security (DHS) in 2003; it was previously in the General Services Administration. FPS employs 1,100 government personnel along with 15,000 contract security guards. However, the group lacks enough people or money to carry out its mission effectively. FPS officials reported the group's total workforce has dropped from 1,400 in fiscal 2004 to 1,100 in fiscal 2007, a decrease of about 20 percent. FPS employs 756 Inspectors and Police Officers and 15,000 contractors to monitor federal facilities.[44] These shortages represent great opportunities for future applicants, as the positions will have to be filled at some point in time.

ICE is a very new organization that came about after the Department of Homeland Security came into being. Currently, ICE has its share of morale and organizational issues because of the turmoil of trying to reorganize the employees that came from its two main founding agencies, the Immigration and Naturalization Service and the Customs Service. If you are willing to put up with an organization with some growing pains, this is a great agency to work for because of its law enforcement mission and worldwide relocation opportunities.

---

[44]HSToday Daily Briefing for Monday, February 11, 2008

The Marshals Service, through three primary positions, protects the federal courts and ensures the effective operation of the judicial system. The Marshal Service is one of the oldest law enforcement agencies in the country and organizationally falls under the Department of Justice. The Marshals Service have a three-tiered workforce model for its operational employees. According to a Marshals Service headquarters official, the Marshals Service took this action to more appropriately match employee skill and pay levels with job tasks after officials recognized the Marshals Service frequently utilized highly trained deputies to perform less complex court related duties, including prisoner detention and transportation. This three-tiered workforce consists of:

1. Detention Enforcement Officers (DEO),
2. Deputy Marshals (DM), and
3. Criminal Investigator Deputy Marshals (CIDM),

With each position having a tailored scope of duties. The duties of these positions become successively broader and more complex. For example, Detention Enforcement Officer responsibilities consist primarily of processing and transporting prisoners. However, Deputy Marshals supervise prisoners during court proceedings and assist Criminal Investigator Deputy Marshals with more complex investigative duties. Further, CIDMs focus their efforts on investigative duties, including surveillance, protective assignments, threats endangering the judicial process, and protection of witnesses. Finally, each position may perform the duties of the lower tier. For example, Deputy Marshals may perform Detention Enforcement Officer duties and Criminal Investigator Deputy Marshals may perform Deputy Marshal and Detention Enforcement Officer assignments.

According to a senior Marshals Service headquarters official, since 2003, most of the Marshals Service's new CIDMs came from the DM ranks. In order for DMs to become CIDMs, they had to compete for available CIDM positions through a formal application process. To be eligible for a CIDM position, applicants were required to have at least one year of experience as a DM and have a performance rating of "acceptable." Additionally, in applying for a CIDM position, DM applicants had to submit a written description of their experience performing or assisting with various Marshals Service activities, including prisoner transportation, court security, fugitive investigations, and protective details.

There are some morale issues in the Marshals Service. One concern is the disparity in pay between the DM and CIDM positions. The predominant criticism expressed is the actual duties performed by DMs and CIDMs did not differ significantly enough to require a distinction between the two positions. DMs stated that, as a result, they often performed the same duties as CIDMs, albeit for less pay.

Another concern commonly expressed is that DMs often are unable to gain the experience necessary to be eligible for a CIDM position. Due to the high demands of the courts in several of the districts, DMs in these districts are spending most of their time handling prisoner transportation and court security. As a result, these DMs often did not perform work in other mission areas, including fugitive investigations and protective details.

In an effort to create a more flexible workforce capable of responding to the full range of mission requirements, the Marshals Service implemented a new directive permitting each DM that meets certain requirements to noncompetitively convert to a CIDM position. According to the Marshals Service, this directive is also designed to:

- ensure that successful participants have the requisite knowledge, skill, and ability to carry out CIDM duties; and
- support the Marshals Service's efforts to attract and retain a workforce capable of meeting the demands presented by the Marshals Service's varying mission activities.

This should help out with some of the previously mentioned issues. As far as overall morale, some Marshals Service operational personnel expressed dissatisfaction with the GS 12 journeyman level of CIDMs. According to these individuals, criminal investigators at other DOJ components, namely the FBI and DEA, attain journeyman status at the GS 13 level. The CIDMs believed their duties were comparable to those performed by Special Agents at these other agencies and thus should be afforded equivalent journeyman level status.[45][46]

Regardless of the pay disparity and any other issues, from my perspective the Marshals Service should be a top choice for any applicant. However, the problem many job seekers will face is getting their foot in the door with this agency: As of October 31, 2006, the Marshals Service no longer accepted requests to take the entry level DM examination. For DM positions, the Marshals Service is currently limited to hiring individuals who:

---

[45]http://www.usdoj.gov/oig/reports/USMS/a0738/chapter4.htm
[46] http://www.opm.gov/oca/wage/index.asp

- Are completing an authorized Cooperative Education Program with the Marshals Service through an accredited College or University;
- Have completed the Federal Career Intern Program (FCIP).
- An applicant must attend an Informational Session Seminar hosted by the participating district. These Seminars are offered on a limited basis during the year. Please check http://www.usmarshals.gov/careers/status.htm for updated seminar information. At the seminar, applicants will be given specific instruction regarding the application process. Qualified candidates will be hired on at the applicable GS 5 and GS 7 level within an Excepted Service status. Upon satisfactory completion of a two year trial period, Deputies will be placed into the Competitive Service status.[47]

National Marine Fisheries Service (NMFS)

The NMFS through its Office for Law Enforcement (OLE) is dedicated primarily to the enforcement of laws that protect and regulate our nation's living marine resources and their natural habitat. This agency is sometimes confused with the FWS, mainly because of their similar names; however the NMFS falls under the National Oceanic and Atmospheric Administration (NOAA) and is not part of the Department of Interior. There are two main law enforcement positions in the NMFS.

1. Enforcement Officers provide the uniformed patrol/inspection arm of the OLE. They monitor vessel offloads, inspect plants and records, and patrol to deter and detect violations.
2. Special Agents perform the investigative function. They investigate complex civil and criminal violations; perform undercover work, and build cases that document complex under-logging, fraud, and misreporting schemes. Community Oriented Policing and Problem Solving and partnerships are important tools used to promote compliance.

NMFS Special Agents and Enforcement Officers conduct complex criminal and civil investigations, board vessels fishing at sea, inspect fish processing plants, review sales of wildlife products on the Internet and conduct patrols on land, in the air and at sea. NMFS Special Agents and Enforcement Officers use patrol vessels to board vessels fishing at sea, and conduct additional patrols on land, in the air and at sea in conjunction with other local, state and federal agencies.[48]

---

[47] http://www.usmarshals.gov/careers/status.htm
[48] http://www.nmfs.noaa.gov/ole/investigations.html

National Park Service (NPS)

There are really two distinct law enforcement positions within the NPS. They are Park Rangers and Park Police Officers. Park Rangers perform a wide variety of duties in managing parks, historical sites, and recreational areas. Park Rangers supervise, manage and perform work in the conservation and use of resources in national parks and other federally managed areas. Park Rangers carry out various tasks associated with forest or structural fire control; protection of property; gathering and dissemination of natural, historical, or scientific information; development of interpretive material for the natural, historical, or cultural features of an era; demonstration of folk art and crafts; enforcement of laws and regulations; investigation of violations, complaints, trespass/encroachment, and accidents; search and rescue; and management of historical, cultural, and natural resources, such as wildlife, forests, lake shores, seashores, historic buildings, battlefields, archaeological properties, and recreation areas.

They also operate campgrounds, including such tasks as assigning sites, replenishing firewood, performing safety inspections, providing information to visitors, and leading guided tours. Differences in the exact nature of duties depend on the grade of position, the site's size and specific needs. Park Rangers work in urban, suburban, and rural areas. More than half of the Park Rangers work in areas east of the Mississippi River. Much of their work is performed outdoors, but often Rangers must work in offices, especially as they advance and assume more managerial responsibilities. During their careers, most Rangers can expect to be assigned to several different parts of the country.[49]

The history of the US Park Police predates both the Department of the Interior and the National Park Service. Created in 1791 by George Washington, the Park Police have been on duty in our federal parks for more than 200 years. The Park Police is now a unit of the Department of the Interior, National Park Service, with jurisdiction in all National Park Service areas and certain other federal and State lands. The primary duty of the Park Police is to protect lives. Park Police Officers are hired by the National Capitol Region and are initially assigned to the metropolitan Washington, D.C., area, where most of the force operates. Police Officers may be assigned to areas in New York City or San Francisco and may be detailed to any park of the National Park System on a temporary basis, but men and women who are considering careers as Park Police Officers should expect to work in a large urban area.

Park Police Officers are more like a big city uniformed police force than any other federal law enforcement agency. They preserve the peace; prevent, detect, and investigate accidents and crimes; aid citizens in emergency situations; arrest violators; and often provide crowd control at large public gatherings. Specialized groups within the Park Police includes; horse mounted, motorcycle, helicopter, and canine units, a special equipment and tactics team, and investigations and security details.

---

[49] http://www.nps.gov/personnel/rangers.htm

Park Police wear an official uniform. In spite of the fact the Park Police Officers work irregular hours and exposed to hazardous and stressful situations, the competition for these jobs is great, and examinations for these positions are not always available. Unless eligible for federal transfer or reinstatement, applicants must pass a written test administered by OPM's Washington, D.C. office. All applicants must be at least 21, but under 37 years old, have good vision, possess or be able to obtain a valid driver's license, pass a physical examination prior to final selection, and undergo a background investigation. The Park Police wants individuals who can exercise mature judgment in applying the law to a variety of situations. The abilities to learn and apply detailed and complex regulations and procedures, to communicate effectively, both orally and in writing, and to keep one's composure under pressure are indicators of successful job performance. Two years of progressively responsible experience demonstrating the types of knowledge, skills, and abilities just described, or the substitution of successfully completed education beyond high school at the rate of one year (30 credits) for every one year experience, qualifies you for entry level consideration.[50]

Secret Service

The Secret Service is one of the most elite law enforcement organizations in the world. It has earned this reputation throughout more than 140 years of unparalleled service to the nation. As one of the oldest federal law enforcement agencies in the country, the Secret Service has dual missions that include investigations as well as protection. These are the unique characteristics that distinguish the Secret Service from other law enforcement organizations. There are two distinct law enforcement positions within the Secret Service;

1. Special Agents, and
2. Uniformed Officers.

Since its inception in 1865, the Secret Service has been involved in protecting the integrity of the nation's financial systems. Recent advances in technology have changed the nature of financial transactions throughout the world. Consequently, the Secret Service's investigative responsibilities have increased significantly.

The Secret Service has jurisdiction in the United States for investigations involving the counterfeiting of United States and foreign obligations and securities. This authority has expanded to include the investigation of financial institution fraud, access device fraud, computer crimes, fraudulent government and commercial securities, fictitious financial instruments, telecommunications fraud, false identification and identity theft. In the years since the Secret Service's protective mission was first mandated in 1901, the agency's jurisdiction has expanded over time and currently includes protection for the following:
- The president, the vice president, (or other individuals next in order of succession to the Office of the President), the president-elect and vice president-elect
- The immediate families of the above individuals;

---

[50]http://www.nps.gov/personnel/parkpolice.htm

- Former presidents, their spouses for their lifetimes, except when the spouse remarries. In 1997, congressional legislation became effective limiting Secret Service protection to former presidents for a period of not more than 10 years from the date the former president leaves office;
- Children of former presidents until age 16;
- Visiting heads of foreign states or governments and their spouses traveling with them, other distinguished foreign visitors to the United States, and official representatives of the United States performing special missions abroad;
- Major presidential and vice presidential candidates, and their spouses within 120 days of a general presidential election;
- Other individuals as designated per Executive Order of the President;
- National Special Security Events, when designated as such by the Secretary of the Department of Homeland Security.

Uniformed Officers of the Secret Service are responsible for providing additional support to the Secret Service's protective mission through the following special support programs:

- The Counter sniper Support Unit (CS): Created in 1971, the CS unit's purpose is to provide specialized protective support to defend against long range threats to Secret Service protectees. Today CS is an operational element of the Presidential Protective Division;
- The Canine Explosives Detection Unit (K-9): Created in 1976, the mission of the K-9 unit is to provide skilled and specialized explosives detection support to protective efforts involving Secret Service protectees;
- The Emergency Response Team (ERT): Formed in 1992, ERT's primary mission is to provide tactical response to unlawful intrusions and other protective challenges related to the White House and its grounds. ERT personnel receive specialized, advanced training and must maintain a high level of physical and operational proficiency;
- Magnetometers: The Secret Service began relying on magnetometer (metal detector) support by Uniformed Division officers to augment its protective efforts away from the White House following the attempted assassination of President Ronald Reagan. The Magnetometer Support Unit's mission is to ensure that all persons entering secure areas occupied by Secret Service protectees are unarmed.

The Secret Service does a pretty good job in comparison to other agencies regarding hiring from the ranks of their Uniformed Officers for Special Agent positions. This is a great opportunity for Uniformed Officers to move up the GS scale and for career advancement. For additional information on applying for a Special Agent or Uniformed Officer position, please follow this link.[51]

Transportation Security Administration (TSA)

TSA employees help secure our transportation infrastructure from future terrorist acts in intelligence, regulation enforcement and inspection positions. The main law enforcement position in TSA is the Federal Air Marshal. Arguably there is a second vital law

---

[51]http://www.ustreas.gov/usss/opportunities.shtml

enforcement component, Security Screeners; however, they do not carry firearms or make arrests.

Federal Air Marshals detect, deter, and defeat hostile acts against United States air carriers, passengers, and crews. They are deployed on passenger flights worldwide to protect airline passengers and crew against the risk of criminal and terrorist violence. Federal Air Marshals perform investigative work and participate in multi-agency task forces and in land based investigative assignments to proactively fight terrorism. Federal Air Marshals provide air security by fighting attacks targeting United States airports, passengers, and crews. They disguise themselves as ordinary passengers and board flights of United States air carriers to locations worldwide. [52] Federal Air Marshals promote public confidence in the safety of the nation's aviation system as a "quiet professional" in the skies.

In response to the attacks of September 11, there was a huge buildup of Federal Air Marshals and many of the employees came from other federal law enforcement jobs in the hopes of finding something better. Some of the new employee that switched to the Air Marshals from other agencies, namely the Border Patrol, found out the grass is not always greener on the other side. The work involves long hours, lots of time away from home, and is very sedentary. As a result, many of these employees are now seeking their new greener pastures.

Transportation Security Offices (Security Screeners) implement security screening procedures that are central to TSA objectives to protect the traveling public by preventing any deadly or dangerous objects from being transported onto an aircraft. They assist in conducting screening of passengers, baggage and cargo as well as monitoring the flow of passengers through the screening checkpoint to facilitate the orderly and efficient processing of passengers.[53]

Although TSA employees are Excepted Service, they currently have a memorandum of agreement signed at the Department Head level that gives all TSA employees the right to Merit Promotion or reassignment within the Department of Homeland Security.

---

[52] http://www.opm.gov/oca/wage/index.asp
[53] http://www.tsa.gov/join/careers/index.shtm

Chapter 4: Federal Salaries

Starting salary is a critical factor for most people in their decision process regarding which jobs to seek. The advertised salary for a federal law enforcement job and the actual expected earned income can be very different because of overtime and other pay compensation. Also, the federal government uses a variety of pay systems for law enforcement employees, some are similar to others and some are very dissimilar from one another. The predominant federal pay system is the General Schedule (GS) although even within the GS system there are special pay provisions that provide higher rates of pay for some law enforcement personnel. For the long term, there is speculation that salaries of federal law enforcement personnel will undergo drastic transformations as the government attempts to become more efficient and effective in motivating and managing its employees. The latest federal pay trend is for "market based" salaries in a system commonly known as "pay banding" or "pay for performance."

In 2007, the standard basic pay systems as identified by OPM for federal law enforcement officers are the GS system and the Federal Wage System[54] (FWS). However, there are numerous nonstandard pay systems currently in use throughout the federal government. The number of officers in standard (GS and FWS) and nonstandard pay systems is as follows: Out of roughly 135,000 total federal law enforcement officers, about 115,500 are covered by the two standard pay systems.

*The information provided in this graph comes from a 2004 OPM report to Congress for the purpose of making recommendations for ensuring, to the maximum extent practicable, the elimination of disparities for law enforcement officers throughout the federal government.

Federal Pay Systems*
For Law Enforcement Officers

All Other
Pay Systems
19,500
14%

GS & FWS
Pay
Systems
115,500
86%

---

[54] The Federal Wage System is a uniform pay-setting system that covers blue-collar workers who are paid by the hour. There are approximately 4,500 federal police officers in this standard system.

The great majority of those employees are in the GS system with the FWS only representing about 4,500 law enforcement employees. Groups covered by nonstandard basic pay systems include about 7,000 officers in the Judicial and Legislative Branches, about 2,000 officers in the Postal Service, about 1,300 Bureau of Diplomatic Security Special Agents who are in the Foreign Service, and about 1,200 Postal Police Officers.[55] These numbers could shift dramatically in the near future as there are changes possible for nearly 55,000 law enforcement personnel mostly from DHS.

GS Scale

Within each grade level, on the GS Scale, there are 10 steps or levels. Pay increases associated with step increases are intended to recognize experience and longevity in your position. The average step increase is roughly equivalent to 3 percent of your basic salary.

Annual Rates by Grade and Step
2020 GS SCALE for WASHINGTON-BALTIMORE
NORTHERN VIRGINIA, DC-MD-PA-VA-WV

Grade	Step 1	Step 2	Step 3	Step 4	Step 5	Step 6	Step 7	Step 8	Step 9	Step
1	$25,500	$26,354	$27,202	$28,045	$28,893	$29,389	$30,227	$31,073	$31,106	$31,
2	$28,672	$29,354	$30,304	$31,106	$31,456	$32,381	$33,306	$34,231	$35,157	$36,
3	$37,539	$38,582	$39,624	$40,667	$41,709	$42,752	$43,794	$44,837	$45,879	$46,
4	$42,141	$43,312	$44,482	$45,652	$46,823	$47,993	$49,164	$50,334	$51,504	$52,
5	$48,462	$47,772	$51,082	$52,392	$53,702	$55,012	$56,322	$57,632	$58,942	$60,
6	$51,099	$52,559	$54,019	$55,479	$56,939	$58,399	$59,859	$61,319	$62,779	$64,
7	$55,158	$56,780	$58,402	$60,023	$61,654	$63,267	$64,889	$66,511	$68,133	$69,
8	$57,495	$59,291	$61,088	$62,885	$64,682	$66,478	$68,275	$70,072	$71,868	$73,
9	$61,519	$63,503	$65,488	$67,473	$69,457	$71,442	$73,426	$75,411	$77,396	$79,
10	$67,747	$69,932	$72,118	$74,303	$76,489	$78,674	$80,860	$83,045	$85,231	$87,
11	$72,030	$74,431	$76,832	$79,233	$81,634	$84,034	$86,435	$88,836	$91,237	$93,
12	$86,335	$89,213	$92,091	$94,970	$97,484	$100,727	$103,605	$106,483	$109,362	$112,
13	$102,663	$106,085	$109,508	$112,930	$116,353	$119,775	$123,198	$126,620	$130,043	$133,
14	$121,316	$125,360	$129,404	$133,447	$137,491	$141,534	$145,578	$149,621	$153,665	$157,
15	$142,701	$147,458	$152,215	$156,973	$161,730	$166,487	$170,800	$170,800	$170,800	$170,

In the GS system, if your performance is rated as satisfactory or higher, you will be granted within grade step increases in pay at the following intervals:

- Steps 1 through 4 occur at one year intervals;
- Steps 5 through 7 occur at two year intervals;
- Steps 8 through 10 occur at three year intervals.

If you have periods of leave without pay (LWOP), it may delay the effective date of your next Within Grade Increase (WGI). If you are promoted to the next higher grade, you

---

[55] http://www.opm.gov/oca/leo_report04/part_III.asp

will receive an increase of at least as much as two steps at your current grade. For example; if you are a GS 6 step 5 on the general schedule and you are promoted to the GS 7, your new salary on the GS 7 scale must meet or exceed the pay of a GS 6 step 7 on the general schedule. In this example, using existing salary tables, you would advance to the GS 7 step 4 pay level.[56]

The GS system also allows law enforcement officers to receive extra compensation in some instances, notably when a job involves hazardous duty. In addition, many federal law enforcement officers receive a substantial percentage increase on top of their base pay for a category of duties known as irregularly scheduled overtime work. That category encompasses administratively uncontrollable overtime pay, which is a discretionary payment of 10 percent to 25 percent for Border Patrol Agents and certain other law enforcement officers, and law enforcement availability pay (LEAP), which is a fixed 25 percent supplement for Special Agents and some other law enforcement personnel. Those payments considerably increase an officer's earned income, although the sum of base pay and differential pay is subject to a pay cap.[57] Some federal officers are also eligible for overtime pay, night-shift differential pay, Sunday pay, and holiday pay. Moreover, OPM has the authority to give special locality payments to certain occupational groups under various circumstances that include problems with recruitment and retention.[58] [59]

To offer more confusion to the already muddled GS system there is a new "GL" pay plan for employees receiving Law Enforcement Officer special base rates, e.g. Border Patrol Agents. After October 1, 2006, any GS employee entitled to a Law Enforcement Officer special base rate at grades GS 3 through GS 10 are assigned a GL pay plan code instead of a GS pay plan code. Note that when a law enforcement officer with a GL pay plan code is promoted to a GS position at the GS 11 grade or higher, the officer's pay plan code is changed to GS.[60]

---

[56] http://nasapeople.nasa.gov/employeebenefits/benefits/handbook/chapter5.htm
[57] 5 U.S.C. §5307.
[58] That authority is provided in 5 U.S.C. §5305(a). According to OPM, fewer than 2 percent of federal law enforcement officers receive those special rates.
[59] http://www.cbo.gov/ftpdocs/66xx/doc6619/08-23-LawEnforcementPay.pdf
[60] http://www.opm.gov/oca/pay/html/specialratechange.asp

The Federal Wage System

The Federal Wage System is a uniform pay-setting system that covers blue-collar workers who are paid by the hour. There are approximately 4,500 federal police officers in this standard system. The system's goal is to ensure that federal trade, craft, and laboring employees within a local wage area who perform the same duties receive the same rate of pay. Under this uniform pay system:

- Your pay will be the same as the pay of other federal jobs like yours in your wage area, and
- Your pay will be in line with pay for private sector jobs like yours in your wage area.[61]

Under the FWS system there are periodic surveys of the local market to adjust the hour rate for wage changes that occur.

Nonstandard Basic Pay Systems

Certain law enforcement officers are covered by basic pay systems that are not among the standard government wide systems (GS or FWS). Congress provided independent authority for these systems. The provisions of these systems may be established directly in law, by administrative action, or by collective bargaining. Following are brief summaries of the major nonstandard basic pay systems for law enforcement personnel.

Judicial Branch Pay Plans

The Judicial Branch has several pay plans that cover probation and pretrial services officers and Supreme Court Police (including the Marshal and Deputy Marshals who supervise those police). The Supreme Court Police pay plan is identical to the pay plan for Capitol Police.

Capitol Police

By law, the basic pay plan for Capitol Police is established and maintained by the Capitol Police Board. The pay schedule for Capitol police is significantly higher than that for GS police officers and is higher than the schedules for Secret Service Uniform Division and Park Police Officers. The Capitol Police have a competitive starting salary of $49,631.00. Upon successful completion of basic training, the salary is increased to $51,370.00. A Private First Class with 30 months of service receives an annual salary of $57,601.00. Basic pay is based on rank with years of total service determining the step rate within the rank. Note: Library of Congress Police Officers eventually will be folded into the Capitol Police force.

---

[61] http://www.opm.gov/oca/wage/index.asp

Postal Service

The Postal Inspection Service has special basic pay systems for Postal Inspectors and executives. The Postal Service also has a separate basic pay authority for its Office of Inspector General. These systems are comparable to the systems that apply to GS Special Agents. Postal Inspectors are exempt from the Fair Labor Standards Act (FLSA) and do not qualify for overtime compensation. Salaries are based on the Inspection Service Law Enforcement (ISLE) pay scale, which corresponds to the GS pay scale for law enforcement officers. Minimum entry base pay levels range from an ISLE 9 step 1 to ISLE 12 step 10. Regarding the uniformed officers of the Postal Service, the Postal Security Force personnel are in a downsizing mode. It is unlikely that you will see any vacancy announcements for these positions.

Transportation Security Administration (TSA)

TSA has a pay banding system for GS equivalent employees, including Federal Air Marshals and Special Agents. Although Federal Air Marshals were detailed to, the Bureau of Immigration and Customs Enforcement they are now back in TSA and remain covered by the TSA pay banding system. These officers are in a specialized law enforcement job category with a specific banding structure. The TSA pay bands are open ranges without the steps of the GS scale. This TSA pay system, which is modeled after the FAA pay plan, has higher pay ranges than the GS system. For Federal Air Marshals in TSA Band I, maximum pay in Washington, DC is currently $96,175, as compared to $93,742 for GS 13 Special Agents (about 3 percent higher, down from a gap of 7 percent prior to the GS adjustment.) In addition, the cap on locality-adjusted rates is the rate for level III of the Executive Schedule (EX-III), as compared to the rate for EX-IV for GS employees. The TSA pay banding system is very similar to the system that has been proposed for many DHS law enforcement agencies and others.

Secret Service Uniformed Division and Park Police

The pay system for Secret Service Uniform Division officers and Park Police Officers provides higher pay than is available for GS police officers. The pay range for Secret Service Uniform Division/Park Police at the Private rank ranges from $46,388.00 to $85,534.00 in Washington, DC. In contrast, the pay range for a GS police officer in Washington, DC, at the most common GS 6 grade, ranges from $40,272 to $52,353. Basic pay is based on rank with step rate within the rank based on years of total service.

Bureau of Diplomatic Security (DS) Special Agents

DS Special Agents in the State Department are covered by the Foreign Service pay system. Starting salaries range from $37,413 to $51,788, depending on qualifications, location of assignment, and related specialized experience. Upon successful completion of all training, Special Agents become eligible for Law Enforcement Availability Pay, equal to a 25 percent increase of their base salary. Satisfactory performance earns employees automatic grade and pay increases during the first 3 years. Thereafter, promotions are competitive based on the recommendations of annual selection panels.[62]

Bureau of Engraving and Printing and Mint Police

The Bureau of Engraving and Printing (BEP) and Mint police officers are covered by a pay system administered by the Secretary of the Treasury (TR scale). The rate of basic pay for these police may not be less than the minimum rate for GS 7 or more than the maximum rate for GS 15. The current BEP/Mint police pay schedule sets pay significantly above GS rates for comparable police officers, but below the rates for Secret Service Uniform Division Officers and Park Police Officers.

Defense Protective Service (DPS) Police

The Secretary of Defense administers a special pay system for Department of Defense (DOD) DPS Police Officers who protect the Pentagon and surrounding areas. DOD has administratively adopted the same pay plan that applies to Secret Service Uniform Division and Park Police Officers.

National Security Agency (NSA) Police

NSA Police Officers are covered by an NSA administered pay plan that generally mirrors the GS system.

Government Printing Office (GPO) Police

The GPO police officers are paid from pay schedules that correspond to GS grades, each with 10 steps like the GS, but with higher pay levels. The normal journey level for GPO police officers is grade 5.

Others

Veterans Administration police who are in the GS pay system but covered by title 38 special rates could also be considered as having a nonstandard system. Among the additional categories of other law enforcement personnel who are covered by nonstandard basic pay systems are Internal Revenue Service Special Agent senior managers and Special Agents in various financial regulatory agencies, such as the Federal

---

[62] http://www.state.gov/m/ds/career/c8853.htm#salary

Deposit Insurance Corporation, the National Zoological Park Police and police employed in various personnel demonstration projects.[63]

Starting Salaries and Pay Ranges

To add confusion to the multiple pay systems used in the federal government is the fact that vacancy announcements advertise a pay range. For example; the starting base pay advertised for a Park Police Officer in 2019 is $54,541. "Yes, I will take the $54,541 starting salary please." The reality is that an agency will likely offer you the lowest base salary listed unless you have previous qualifying experience or a unique skill. However, my experience is the advertised lowest starting base salary for a federal law enforcement job gives a false bad impression. In other words, you will make more money than the minimum base salary indicated because of differential pay, overtime pay, Sunday pay, and holiday pay.

Certainly, when dealing with pay systems that provide automatic progressions for longevity, like the GS system, your salary over the first few years will dramatically increase. For example; an entry level position as a CBP Officer (formerly Customs Inspector) may have a progression from GS 5, to GS 7, to GS 9, with the journeyman grade being a GS 11. Based on the 2020 GS schedule for the Washington DC area, that employee will have a base pay of $48,462 the first year. In the beginning of the employees fourth year, the base pay should be $61,519, almost double the initial salary.

The yearly grade increases, are almost automatic, similar to step increases. In theory, they can be denied for performance and conduct issues; in practice, denying grade or step increase is rare. However, the advertised salary range does not include very lucrative overtime incentives. CBP Officers are paid "double time" when they work more than eight hours a day or on a federal holiday. This money can be substantial. In fact, Congress has capped CBP Officers' overtime at $30,000.

Grade Creep

Grade creep is an artificial inflation (creeping higher) of grades without an accompanying rise in the difficulty and responsibility of work. This phenomenon is worth mentioning because of its impact on law enforcement salaries. For example, in the early 1980's most Special Agent positions had a journeyman grade of GS 12. The FBI was able to raise the grade of their journeyman Special Agents to the GS 13 level. Once the FBI was able to open that door, other agencies wanted the same grade for their own agents and without it; there are real problems with retention and recruiting. Eventually, most other agencies followed suit and were able to match the FBI's grade increase. In the late 1990, most Special Agents were also granted an automatic 25% increase to their base pay.

---

[63] http://www.opm.gov/oca/leo_report04/part_III.asp

While it could be argued the duties of these law enforcement officers actually became more complex because of computer technology and other changes, I would propose there are other factors at work. Given the laws of supply and demand, agency heads are under a lot of pressure to attract and recruit the best and brightest employees. Specifically, it seems that occupational grade increases occur first in agencies and positions with more political influence, i.e., the FBI and Secret Service Special Agents. My observation from anecdotal evidence is that smaller and lesser-known agencies and positions tend to be left back and are well behind the power curve in this game. Given the choice, prudent job applicants should pursue the more prestigious and politically attuned agencies if they want to an innovative beneficiary of grade creep.

The Future of Federal Salaries

The good news is the Feds are trying to standardize the various pay systems to create parity among the different law enforcement agencies. In a few years it is likely that pay banding will be the new "standard" system in the federal government mainly because of the flexibility it offers management. There is a very strong push at high levels of the government to use an alternative to the GS pay systems for federal law enforcement officers. The best evidence of this is occurring in the Department of Homeland Security (DHS), which contains the single largest group of law enforcement officers in the federal government.

> In April 2003, the Secretary of DHS and the Director of OPM assembled a design team composed of DHS managers and employees, Human Resources (HR) experts from DHS and OPM, and representatives from the agency's three largest unions. The design team's mission was to develop a broad range of alternatives to the current GS pay tables used by the federal government that improve the efficiency and effectiveness of hiring and retaining DHS employees....[64]

One of the recommendations of the design team's proposal was a pay banding system. Pay banding as it is proposed by DHS is similar to the GS scale except that pay increases are directly tied to performance rather than longevity. The implementation of the new pay system throughout DHS has been slowed mainly because of legal challenges by employee unions. Although there is much concern among GS employees that pay banding will deteriorate their salaries in the long term, there is evidence to the contrary. An article in by Ralph Smith in the Friday, January 25, 2008 edition of Fedsmith.com provides more insight on this issue.

---

[64] http://www.dhs.gov/xlibrary/assets/privacy/privacy_pia_ochcoreward.pdf

Bottom Line

Yes, federal salaries are confusing because there is inconsistency between agency pay systems. Many experts now agree the standard GS system, which is based on an industrial age workforce rather than an information age workforce, should be overhauled. With all the nonstandard pay systems and special pay benefits it is hard for someone new to the government to accurately predict how much earned income to expect in their first year on the job. If the base pay is truly a legitimate concern, you may want to inquire about this with a recruiter at the agency.

If you are looking to make a lot of money during a career, law enforcement is not the job for you. The white-collar (Special Agent) jobs generally pay more than blue-collar (uniformed officers) jobs. Many people come to the realization early in their career that money and job satisfaction are not necessarily one in the same. The Feds usually make more money than their non-federal law enforcement counterparts do. The exception to that rule may be law enforcement positions in a few major metropolitan areas.[65]

---

[65] http://www.cbo.gov/ftpdocs/66xx/doc6619/08-23-LawEnforcementPay.pdf

Chapter 5: Retirement and Other Benefits

Federal retirement and other benefits are a significant reason for many to seek careers with the government. People often want federal employment after a bad experience with the private sector; i.e., downsizing, layoffs, outsourcing, or a corporate bankruptcy. The federal government does offer a very good retirement and benefits package compared to most other similar employers. New employees coming into the federal government for the first time come under the umbrella of the Federal Employees Retirement System (FERS). In theory, FERS retirees will receive money from three separate and unique sources:

1. Federal Pension;
2. Thrift Savings Plan (TSP);
3. And Social Security.

I say "in theory" because the continued solvency of the Social Security system for the baby-boom generation is open to debate. If it survives at all, Social Security benefits for retirees will likely be substantially reduced in the not so distant future. As bad as that may seem, the FERS system is still better than what is offered by much of the corporate world. Many companies are eliminating their pension plans in favor of only offering 401K plans. The good news, for the time being, is the Feds have both plans. A pension plan and the TSP, which is essentially a 401K, plan (individual retirement account). Having identified that potential pitfall with Social Security, here is what the Feds have to say about FERS.

The FERS is an outstanding three-tiered plan to provide secure retirement, disability and survivor benefits for employees and their dependents. In addition to Social Security benefits as a base, FERS offers both an annuity that grows with length of service and a tax deferred savings plan. Employees pay less than one percent of salary to qualify for the annuity and are fully vested after five years of service and, for disability benefits, after just 18 months. (5 CFR part 843) See also http://www.opm.gov/asd/ and http://www.opm.gov/retire/index.htm.[66]

FERS Immediate Retirement Age

An immediate retirement is the term used when an employee works a full career and then retires as opposed to disability, early, and deferred retirements. There are two distinct methods for calculating immediate retirement ages, one for 6C-covered positions and one for non-covered positions. Remember that covered positions must meet a strict OPM definition of law enforcement.

---

[66] http://www.opm.gov/account/omsoe/hr-flex/HR_flex.txt

Calculating the minimum retirement age (MRA) for covered positions is very simple. Employees receive an unreduced benefit at age 50 with 20 years of service, or at any age with 25 years of service. You also receive a Special Retirement Supplement until age 62 that approximates the Social Security benefit earned in federal service. After you reach the MRA, if you have earnings from wages or self-employment that exceeds the Social Security annual exempt amount, your supplement will be reduced or stopped. In addition, you are entitled to an annual Cost-of-Living Adjustment (COLA), regardless of your age.[67] This means at age 50 with 20 years of service or at any age with 25 years of service, a 6C covered employee can retire. At age 57, retirement is mandatory.

The retirement age for non-covered employees is more complicated to explain. Your age and number of years of creditable service determine eligibility. You must have reached the MRA to receive retirement benefits. Use the following chart to determine your MRA.

If you were born	Your MRA is
Before 1948	55
In 1948	55 and 2 months
In 1949	55 and 4 months
In 1950	55 and 6 months
In 1951	55 and 8 months
In 1952	55 and 10 months
In 1953 through 1964	56
In 1965	56 and 2 months
In 1966	56 and 4 months
In 1967	56 and 6 months
In 1968	56 and 8 months
In 1969	56 and 10 months
In 1970 and after	57

If you meet one of the following sets of age and service requirements, you are entitled to an immediate retirement benefit:

Age	Years of Service
62	5
60	20
MRA	30
MRA	10

If you retire at the MRA with at least 10, but less than 30 years of service, your benefit will be reduced by 5 percent a year for each year you are under 62, unless you have 20 years of service and your benefit starts when you reach age 60 or later.

---

[67] http://www.opm.gov/forms/pdfimage/RI90-1.pdf

Retirement pension benefits for federal workers are based on two factors: Their length of service and the mean average of their highest three years' salary. Most private companies, if they have a pension plan at all, use a high five-year average.[68] A federal pension provides a monthly annuity to the employee or surviving spouse. The immediate retirement annuity starts within 30 days from the date you stop working. This chart shows the percentage value of base pay FERS employees receive from their pension plan after retiring with a given number of years of service. LEO stands for Law Enforcement Officer (as recognized by OPM). Obviously, it pays to be in an OPM recognized law enforcement position, the higher of the two lines. The value of Thrift Savings Plan and Social Security benefits are not shown.

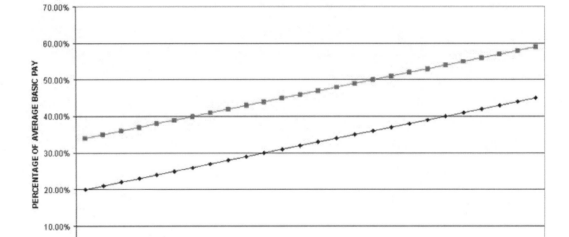

LEO vs. NON-LEO (FERS)

[68]http://www.washingtontimes.com/apps/pbcs.dll/article?AID=/20071120/NATION06/111200068&template=nextpage

The chart below shows the yearly dollar value of FERS pension plan given a number of years of service. The employee's high three years of income are averaged and used in a formula to determine the annuity. The annual annuity rates shown in this chart are derived from the 2001-2003 average pay of a GS 13/7 in the Washington-Baltimore, DC-MD-VA-WV locality pay area. The 2001-2003 average pay of a non-LEO GS 13/7, or a LEO GS 13/7 without availability pay in the Washington-Baltimore locality pay area was $79,399. The 2001-2003 average pay of a GS 13/7 Special Agent receiving LEAP pay in the Washington-Baltimore locality pay area was $99,249. As in the previous chart, the value of Thrift Savings Plan and Social Security benefits are not shown.

EXAMPLE: GS-13 LEO vs. NON-LEO ANNUITIES (FERS)

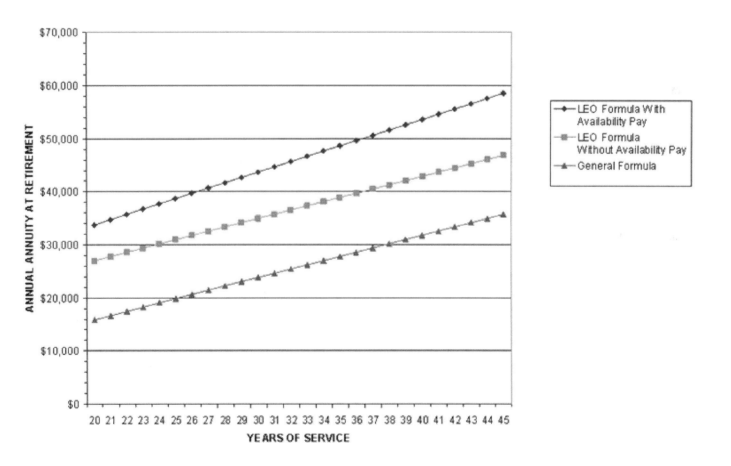

Thrift Savings Plan (TSP)

The TSP is a retirement savings and investment plan for federal employees. Congress established the TSP in the Federal Employees' Retirement System Act of 1986. The purpose of the TSP is to provide retirement income. The TSP offers federal employees the same type of savings and tax benefits that many private corporations offer their employees under 401(k) plans. For a new employee, the TSP is one of the three parts of the retirement package, along with the FERS Basic Annuity and Social Security. Participating in the TSP does not affect the amount of your Social Security benefit or your FERS Basic Annuity (pension). The money that you save and earn through your TSP account will provide an important source of retirement income. As a FERS employee, you may begin contributing to the TSP when you are first hired by the federal government. Once you become eligible for agency contributions, you will receive Agency Automatic (1%) Contributions whether or not you are contributing to your account. If you are contributing to your account, you will also receive Agency Matching Contributions at that time. These matching contributions are a principal benefit of the TSP.

Federal income taxes are deferred on all contributions to your TSP account. To learn more about this important feature, see "Tax Advantages of the TSP." Your TSP benefits can significantly increase your retirement income, but starting early is important. If you start to contribute to your TSP account as soon as you are hired, the earnings in your account will compound over a longer period of time. In addition, if you make certain to contribute your own money early on, you will not miss Agency Matching Contributions once you become eligible for them. To learn how your account could grow, use the calculator "Projecting Your Account Balance."[69]

Other Federal Retirement Systems

It is worth noting there are other federal retirement systems. None of the other systems is now available to an employee that is new to the federal government. The Civil Service Retirement System (CSRS) covered federal employees first hired before January 1, 1984, who were eligible for retirement coverage. Employees first hired on or after January 1, 1984, were automatically covered by FERS. Some employees transferred from CSRS to FERS during a one-time open season period.

A few of my current coworkers are in the CSRS and others are in the DC Fire and Police retirement system. In fact, my father retired under the CSRS system. The main difference is the CSRS federal pension is greater than FERS given the same amount of years of service and retirement age. However, because CSRS employees have not contributed into the Social Security system, CSRS employees are not entitled to a Social Security retirement benefits. In addition, CSRS employees can contribute to the TSP but do not receive any agency matching contributions.

---

[69] http://tsp.gov/features/chapter01.html#sub2

While most Park Police Officers, Secret Service Uniformed Division Officers and Secret Service Special Agents are covered by FERS, there are probably less than 200 Secret Service employees currently covered by the DC Police Officers' and Firefighters' Retirement Plan (DCPOFP). Before FERS was established, Park Police Officers and Secret Service Uniform Division officers were covered by DCPOFP. In addition, CSRS covered Secret Service Special Agents are eligible to transfer to DCPOFP (based on having 10 or more years of service directly related to the protection of the President). The FERS LEO provisions cover new Park Police Officers, Secret Service Uniform Division officers, and Secret Service Special Agents, hired after January 1, 1984.[70]

Many of the former Park Police Officers that I work with have retired under the DCPOFP retirement system. These retired Park Police Officers have the advantage of being able to collect their DCPOFP pension check and begin a new job working for the Feds without any penalty. It seems strange that an employer, Uncle Sam, would pay someone a retirement check and give him or her a paycheck. This is referred to as "double dipping." Potentially my retired Park Police coworkers will receive a second retirement for their current employment and be permanent double dippers. Yes, it pays to know the systems.

Holidays

There is good news and bad news when it comes to federal Holidays. The good news first: Full-time federal employees are entitled to ten paid holidays each year. These holidays are specified in 5 U.S.C. 6103 and are listed by year on OPM's Web site at http://www.opm.gov/fedhol/index.htm. (5 U.S.C. 6301; Executive Order 11582; 5 CFR 610.201, and 610.202)[71]

Calendar Year Federal Holidays

Tuesday, January 1	**New Year's Day**
Monday, January 21	**Birthday of Martin Luther King, Jr.**
Monday, February 18	**Washington's Birthday**
Monday, May 26	**Memorial Day**
Friday, July 4	**Independence Day**
Monday, September 1	**Labor Day**
Monday, October 13	**Columbus Day**
Tuesday, November 11	**Veterans Day**
Thursday, November 27	**Thanksgiving Day**
Thursday, December 25	**Christmas Day**

The bad news regarding federal holidays is that many law enforcement officers, particularly those working at prisons, the border, or protective and security operations

---

[70] http://www2.opm.gov/oca/leo_report04/part_ii.asp#b

[71] http://www.opm.gov/account/omsoe/hr-flex/HR_flex.txt

will likely be required to work during holidays. The unseen benefit to the bad news is that employees are well compensated for having to work on a holiday. Because working a holiday involves overtime pay there are usually at least a few volunteers. Most agencies have well established rules in place for the equitable distribution of overtime when there are no volunteers.

Life Insurance

Most full-time and part-time employees are automatically enrolled in Basic Life Insurance equal to their salary, rounded to the next $1,000, plus $2,000. The government pays ⅓ of the cost of this group term insurance. Employees do not have to prove insurability no physical is required. Basic coverage includes double benefits for accidental death and benefits for dismemberment. Employees can also purchase Optional Insurance at their own expense. Optional coverage includes additional insurance on the employee's life as well as coverage for the employee's spouse and eligible children, if any. Accelerated death benefits are available to terminally ill enrollees so they can receive life insurance proceeds while they are living.

Many large organizations are cutting life insurance benefits to retirees. This is untrue in the federal government where life insurance coverage can be continued into retirement. It can also be converted to private coverage upon termination, without proof of insurability. (5 CFR part 870) See also http://www.opm.gov/insure/. In addition, to offering the life insurance program, agencies can pay up to $10,000 as a death gratuity to the personal representatives of employees who die from injuries sustained in the line of duty.

Health Insurance

Health insurance is becoming a major factor that causes people to seek federal employment. Federal employees can enroll in health insurance coverage for themselves and their families at reasonable rates. They enjoy one of the widest selections of plans in the country. Employees can choose among fee for service plans, health maintenance organizations, and point of service plans. Employees can change their enrollment during an annual open season. Unlike a growing number of private sector health benefits programs, federal employees can continue their health insurance coverage into retirement with full government contribution. Most enrollees pay just about ¼ of the health benefits premium. (5 CFR part 890) See also http://www.opm.gov/insure/.

Federal workers with a family of two (husband and wife) pay the same premiums as a family of 15 or more if they are in the same federal family health plan. Their out of pocket costs will differ dramatically, but they pay the same premiums regardless of family size. When children who have been part of the family plan turn 22, they cease to be dependents. They are no longer part of the family health plan even if they are still dependents or in school. Children who are disabled can be covered by the family plan for life, but for most people, 22 is the departure point. The good news/bad news is the 22 and up children of Feds and retirees can continue to keep coverage (on their own) for up to 36 months. The bad news is that unlike their parents' plan, the government will not pay the lion's share (roughly 72 percent) of the total premium. As a result they will wind up paying anywhere from $3,000 to $6,000 next year, depending on the plan they choose.

Divorced spouses of federal workers and retirees without a court order can also qualify for up to 36 months of coverage in the Federal Employees Health Benefits Program. In most cases, the group rate they will pay under the federal health program will be less than what an individual (and often inferior) plan would cost. Former spouses who have a qualifying court order can continue indefinitely under the federal health plan.[72]

Long Term Care Insurance

With the Long Term Care Security Act, long-term care insurance became a reality for federal employees, members of the military, retirees and their families. It is the first new benefit offered to federal employees since the inception of the Federal Employees Retirement System, with its Thrift Savings Plan component, in June 1986. It provides coverage for long-term care health care needs, such as nursing home care, home health care, assisted living facilities, adult day care, and personal care/homemaker care. See also http://www.opm.gov/insure/ltc/index.htm.

Liability Insurance

A recently enacted law (section 642 of Public Law 106-58) requires federal agencies to reimburse law enforcement officers, supervisors and managers for up to ½ of the cost of professional liability insurance, protecting them from potential liability and attorney's fees for actions arising out of the conduct of official duties.

Severance Pay

Employees under qualifying appointments with at least 12 months of continuous service are eligible for severance pay upon removal from federal service by involuntary separation (excluding removal due to unacceptable performance or conduct). (5 U.S.C. 5595; 5 CFR part 550, subpart G)

Lump Sum Annual Leave Payments

---

[72]http://www.washingtontimes.com/apps/pbcs.dll/article?AID=/20071120/NATION06/111200068&template=nextpage

An employee will receive a lump sum payment for any unused annual leave when he or she separates from federal service or enters on active duty in the armed forces and elects to receive a lump sum payment. Generally, a lump sum payment will equal the pay the employee would have received had he or she remained employed until expiration of the period covered by the annual leave. Additional information on lump sum annual leave payments is found at http://www.opm.gov/oca/leave/HTML/lumpsum.htm. (5 U.S.C. 5551; 5 CFR part 550, subpart L)[73]

---

[73] http://www.opm.gov/account/omsoe/hr-flex/HR_flex.txt

Chapter 6: Vacancy Announcements and Agency Hiring Flexibilities

The most common way to get a federal job is to first apply through a vacancy announcement. A vacancy announcement is the government's way of publicly informing potential applicants of job openings. Hiring flexibilities are methods used in conjunction with a vacancy announcement to select and appoint a person into a position. Much of the information on hiring flexibilities in this document was derived from a report by OPM intended to educate agency hiring officials so they may take advantage of the various hiring authorities available to them. Although OPM often uses the words "hiring flexibilities," the hiring officials within agencies sometimes view the hiring system as inflexible.

Entry Level vs. Career Advancement

Definitions for "entry level" and "career advancement" positions will vary depending upon perspective. From my point of view, law enforcement entry-level positions are jobs that are usually filled by persons from outside the hiring agency. In contrast, career advancement positions are those positions usually filled internally with a Merit Promotion Vacancy Promotion Announcement, from within the same agency or a closely related agency, i.e., ICE and CBP. In addition, career advancement positions are likely to require previous work experience. Some Special Agent positions at entry-level GS grades also have this requirement.

The main difference between entry level and career advancement positions is how the agency announces and fills the vacancy. There is no distinguishing phrase or check mark on a vacancy announcement to inform you the position is either entry level or career advancement. Unfortunately, many job seekers waste a lot of time and effort by unwittingly going through the process of applying for career advancement positions that for all practical purposes are unattainable because they lack the experience. These applicants would have better spent the application postage stamp money on a lottery ticket.

My advice on how to tell the difference between the two types of positions: Typically, career advancement positions will have a prefix to the normal title such as "Senior" or "Supervisory"; however, the telltale sign is when the starting salary is noticeably high. On the other hand, entry-level jobs typically will have multiple grades or pay bands listed such as GS 5/7/9/11 rather than one grade such as GS 13. There are exceptions to the guidelines above. One exception is that when an agency undergoes large hiring increases, such as the Federal Air Marshals immediately after September 11, 2001, they are more likely to hire applicants from outside the agency into career advancement positions. However, those situations are infrequent and when they occur you will need prior law enforcement experience.

In the old days, potential applicants would look for paper copies of vacancy announcements at the post office or other government offices. Now days, almost all job openings are best accessed through the Internet. The federal application process is in a transition with regard to the application process and required resume. Twenty years ago, the Standard Form (SF) 171 seemed to be the only document agencies accepted as a resume. Anyone who has ever completed the SF 171 will tell you that it is a lengthy and cumbersome form to use. The OF 612, another federal resume form, came about to simplify the federal resume. As an option to the OF 612, many agencies also began accepting standard business resumes like those you would prepare for a private sector jobs. The latest trend, and one which is likely to flourish, is a web based job application with resumes and corresponding documents all done via the Internet on systems such as QuickHire®.

When an agency recruits for one or more positions, there are a number of managerial decisions made regarding how the vacancy is advertised. Potential job seekers have no control over these decisions; however, the decisions that are made do give general indications as to the intentions of the agency's management. For example, when a Merit Promotion Vacancy Announcement is open for a short duration (five days), and only open to the originating agency's personnel, it is likely the agency has some of their own people in mind for the position. In contrast, if a vacancy announcement is open for a very long time and advertised as All Sources, there is a good likelihood that no one has the "inside track" for the job.

Applying for federal law enforcement positions has changed dramatically within the last decade due to the widespread use and acceptance of the Internet. Although the process has become digitalized and access to job information is nearly instantaneous, the Feds have held tightly to many of the old forms and methods of evaluating job applicants. The federal government tries to represent itself as one employer. Although Uncle Sam is ultimately where the pay check comes from, the reality is there are over a hundred different law enforcement agencies that have various degrees of autonomy over who and how they hire. These agencies have the freedom to work within an established set of rules to hire an employee, but the rules allow for different hiring processes. There are two all-encompassing categories of vacancy announcements:

1. All Sources Vacancy Announcements, and
2. Merit Promotion Vacancy Announcements.

All Sources means just what it sounds like, it is open to everyone. In contrast, Merit Promotion Vacancy Announcements are only open to persons with specific prior federal qualifications. Merit Promotion Vacancy Announcements have many variations but it is easier to think of it as one category. To use an analogy, All Sources Vacancy Announcements are like public golf courses, they are accessible to everyone. Merit Promotion Vacancy Announcements are like private golf courses, only members and special friends of members can play.

All Sources Vacancy Announcements

All Sources Vacancy Announcements can be open for almost any length of time. The time can be as short as five days or as long as "open continuous" which really means it is kept open until the agency decides to close the announcement. All Sources applicants must receive numerical ratings between 70 and 100 to pass a competitive examination. Regarding scores below 70, as they say in Monopoly "do not pass go, do not collect $200." The reality is that for any position with many applicants you will probably need a score in the 90's or higher. Applicants who are entitled to Veterans Preference have 5 or 10 points added to their earned passing scores. Some veterans could achieve a score of 110. Candidates are then referred to selecting officials in the numerical rank order of their earned scores. The highest scores are first except that compensable disabled veterans are placed above all other candidates. Veterans are always referred ahead of nonveterans with equal scores on an All Sources Vacancy Announcement competitive certificate.[74] There are not a fixed number of names for an All Sources Competitive Certificate; rather, the size is based on the number of applicants and positions to be filled as well as natural break points when comparing applicants' examination scores.

It can be disconcerting to nonveterans that apply to All Sources Vacancy Announcements when they first find out that certain veterans will automatically be given extra points or preference on their examination. As a nonveteran, it is easy to come to terms with this given an understanding and appreciation of the sacrifices our military personnel have made for our country. For those that do not like the veteran's preference, there really is no choice in the matter as it is the law of the land.

Merit Promotion Vacancy Announcements

With respect to the length of time the announcement is open, Merit Promotion Vacancy Announcements are the same as All Sources. However, the main difference is that Merit Promotion Vacancy Announcements place constraints on who can apply. Some special category persons can always apply to any Merit Promotion Vacancy Announcement regardless of certain other restrictions. These special category applicants include Americans with Disabilities Act (ADA), Career Transition Assistance Plan (CTAP), Interagency Career Transition Assistance Plan (ICTAP), 30% Disabled Veterans, and Veterans' Recruitment Appointment (VRA). Usually, Merit Promotion Vacancy Announcements are open to career and career conditional employees of the agency doing the hiring but sometimes a Merit Promotion Vacancy Announcement will only allow

---

[74] http://www.opm.gov/account/omsoc/hr-flex/HR_flex.txt

applicants from the special categories. Merit Promotion Vacancy Announcements can be open broadly to include employees in all civilian federal agencies and the special categories previously mentioned.

Under current regulations, applicants must meet time in grade requirements before applying for Merit Promotion Vacancy Announcements. This means that employees in the Competitive Service GS positions at grades 5 and above must serve 52 weeks in grade before becoming eligible for promotion to the next grade level. One notable exception to this is disabled veterans to apply for any Merit Promotion Vacancy Announcement regardless of time in grade.

One method that agencies use to hire someone that does not qualify for a promotion due to time in grade requirements is to announce the position as a multiple graded job. For example, a Division Chief's position at the Federal Law Enforcement Training Center is normally announced as a straight GS 15 grade level. However, if the decision makers have their eye on someone for the job who does not have the time in grade there is a way to beat the system. The Division Chiefs job can be advertised as a GS 14/15, which makes the minimum acceptable time in grade 52 weeks as a GS 13. When you see, a career advancement job advertised with multiple grades, there might be someone with an inside track for the job. If that someone were yourself, you would probably already know it.

Considering there are already ways around the rules it seems odd that OPM has proposed a rule change regarding Merit Promotions and time in grade requirements. There is a proposal to abolish the 52-week service requirement. The time in grade restrictions were first put into place back in the 1950's as a direct result of the Korean War. There was a real concern by Congress that federal employees would too quickly advance through federal pay levels. This phenomenon had occurred during World War II. The law establishing the time in grade requirement was never renewed after it expired in 1978.

The time in grade requirement continues today because of an OPM regulation. OPM says, "Eliminating the time in grade requirement will not eliminate the agency's determination on whether a candidate is qualified to perform the essential higher level duties. Rather, elimination of the 52 week time in grade waiting period reinforces the principle that promotions are based on an individual's ability to perform the requirements of the position (i.e., Merit) not longevity." This in fact follows the philosophy of pay for performance, which is the current federal trend. In 1996, a similar proposal was made to eliminate the time in grade requirement but it never came to fruition.[75]

---

[75]New Pay-For-Performance Twist Coming to Your Agency By Ralph Smith Friday, February 8, 2008, http://www.fedsmith.com/article/1506/

USAJobs

http://www.USAJobs.opm.gov is the federal government's centralized one stop shopping service for federal vacancy announcements (Merit Promotion and All Sources) and various items of relevant employment. This service is available 24 hours 7 days a week. When doing Internet searches for vacancy announcements, users of search engines such as Google can use the data feed from USAJobs, the government's central jobs portal, to get information that was previously available only through a keyword search on the USAJobs Web site.[76] However, the best method used by most applicants is to go directly to USAJobs.com for your search. Because agency job postings and employment information are located in one government wide system, it saves considerable time and resources for both the potential employee and the various federal agencies. USAJobs is accessible through two delivery systems in which vacancy announcements and employment information are available to all job seekers:

- Web site at http://www.USAJobs.opm.gov/
- USAJobs by Phone at 478/757-3000 (478/744-2299 TDD)

USAJobs offers a variety of features to support recruiting efforts of federal agencies:

- A wide array of job searches including one for student employment opportunities.
- Employment information fact sheets on a wide variety of topics related to federal employment issues, which include agency specific fact sheets.

USAJobs by E-mail features a capability for job seekers to specify up to three customized job searches and then receive an automatic e-mail when new jobs are posted that match those search criteria. The e-mails provide links directly to the vacancy announcements. The Hot Jobs area is available to agencies for posting jobs that are critical or hard to fill. This provides essential visibility to job seekers one click from the home page. USAJobs has a resume builder feature that allows individuals to create, save, update, print, and even submit resumes online. Applicants can use this feature to build a resume and then print it for mailing. In many cases, they can submit them to the hiring agencies online.

Studentjobs.gov provides a one stop shopping service that is strictly for student opportunities within the federal government. It includes links to the student search, USAJobs by e-mail, the resume builder, and many agency profile articles and web pages. Under continuing efforts to modernize and streamline the hiring process, OPM encourages agencies to accept job applications and resumes electronically.[77]

It is critical to read and follow the instructions listed in the vacancy announcement to ensure you are providing the information that is required. Having been on many rating and ranking panels that provide scores to applicants' KSAs, it was common to see

---

[76]*USAJobs links up with major search engines* by Richard W. Walker , 12/6/2007, www.FCW.com
[77] http://www.opm.gov/account/omsoe/hr-flex/HR_flex.txt   most of the text on this page is taken directly from this OPM document.

applications, which did not contain specific information such as written facts addressing the topic in the KSA. Failure to supply the information requested usually results in the applicant not receiving the assessment score they deserved. If this happens to you, it means that your name will likely not show up on the certificate and you do not get any further consideration. Certificates derived by the examination process often contain very high scores and scores that are equal. For All Sources Competitive Examination certificates (but not Merit Promotion), veterans typically receive bonus points that are added to their assessment score. These points are dependent upon their specific veterans' preference status.

The Feds ask you to remain alert for counterfeit "phishing" e-mails that may appear to come from Monster.com asking you to click on a link. According to Monster.com, USAJobs will **NEVER** request personal information via unsolicited e-mail, i.e., not a response to an e-mail sent by you. Monster has also made assurances they will never ask any site users to download any software, "tool" or "access agreement." Please also be on the alert for fraudulent e-mails that advertises positions managing financial transactions, or cashing checks. These e-mails are attempting to engage job seekers in a money laundering or bad check fraud. If you receive a suspicious e-mail regarding your USAJobs search, e-mail it, with the full "header" information intact, to mayday@fedjobs.gov.

Hiring Authorities

Hiring authorities specifically means sanctioned methods that can be used to hire an employee. Federal agencies have many different specific hiring authorities available to them. The federal hiring rules are unlike the corporate world where a company may choose to hire nearly anyone they wish.[78] In the federal Competitive Service world, an applicant has to fit into one of the approximately dozen hiring authorities to be hired. The good news is there are plenty of jobs and numerous hiring authorities. The bad news is there are realistically only a couple usable hiring authorities for persons without federal work experience. To top that off, OPM has recently issued guidance to agencies to stop using the Outstanding Scholar and Bilingual/Bicultural programs.

To make sense of the various hiring authorities it is better to think about the hiring authorities as fitting into two groupings:
1. those that require previous federal experience, and
2. those that do not.

Keep in mind that Excepted Service agencies do not have to use these hiring authorities but often use processes that mimic them. To visually depict the current hiring authorities, I have used two firearms target diagrams indicating a variety of methods available to persons seeking federal law enforcement employment. Current and former federal employees (military and civilian) will have access to qualify for hiring authorities in both diagrams while persons with no prior federal experience will only have access to those authorities listed in the first diagram. All job applicants should be familiar with the hiring flexibilities listed in both diagrams so they will know exactly how the hiring game is played. The knowledge of the "big picture" will help job seekers develop individualized application strategies.

---

[78] Non Federal employers must abide by EEOC rules but not civil service hiring rules.

Veterans
Employment
Opportunities
Act

Veterans
Preferance

Veterans
Recruitment
Appointment

Merit Competitive
Examination

Reinstatement
Eligibles

Displaced
Employees

Merit Promotion

A Merit Promotion is one of the most often-used appointment authorities in the federal government. It is primarily for jobs that are considered career advancement although it is sometimes used for entry-level positions. This is the hiring authority normally used with a Merit Promotion Vacancy Announcement. When used for entry-level positions the purpose is often to hire current agency employees that are in positions that do not provide much career advancement opportunity. To qualify for this hiring authority an applicant must have career or career conditional status. There are other special exceptions to this rule and are covered under other areas in this Chapter, e.g., Displaced Employees, and Disabled Veterans. Employees in the Competitive Service (most of the Executive Branch except the Department of State and FBI) gain career conditional status immediately after they have completed a probationary period and are in a permanent competitive appointment. Career status is acquired after three continuous years of career conditional status.

Merit Promotions represent great opportunities for nonveteran federal employees because the numbers of applicants are limited and veteran's preference points are not added to veterans' examination scores. Sometimes agencies impose strict distance and agency/department limitations on who can apply. Depending on your perspective, this can be good or bad. While in basic training, I was told by my class coordinator there were only three things real in the world, Santa, the Easter Bunny, and Merit Promotion. Obviously my coordinator was somewhat jaded by his Merit Promotion experiences but overall I have found them to be very fair.

Reinstatement Eligibles

The Reinstatement Eligibles Hiring authority is sometimes referred to as the voluntary applicant file (VAF). To use the VAF, an agency voluntarily accepts resumes from applicants wanting to transfer. This hiring authority allows an agency to select someone that meets the minimum job requirements if they have held the same or higher pay grade as the position being selected. In addition, certain veterans are eligible for the Reinstatement Eligibles Hiring Authority. They include 30% or more Disabled Veterans that are eligible for any grade level, and Veterans' Recruitment Appointment that are eligible to apply for jobs up to GS 11.

Surplus and Displaced Employees

Some very good employees find their way to federal jobs because of corporate downsizing. Unfortunately, the Feds also go through periods of restructuring and downsizing. Some federal employees find themselves having to "transition" to new jobs. Sometimes even to occupations in the private sector. This is unlikely to happen in federal law enforcement jobs that involve criminal investigation or border security, as they are considered inherently governmental and a growth industry for years to come.

Yet, in years past, some federal police jobs that involved building security or civil (non-criminal) investigations have been contracted to private sector companies. Other federal job sectors may see this happen to a greater degree, particularly when Uncle Sam is tightening his belt. When that happens, Executive Branch agencies must provide career transition assistance to employees affected by downsizing or restructuring. Career Transition Assistance Plans (CTAPs) for surplus and displaced employees consist of three parts:

1. Agency Career Transition Services - Each agency provides career transition services to surplus employees, giving them skills and resources to help them find other employment. These services might include skills assessment, resume preparation, counseling, or job search assistance. Agencies must also develop policies on retraining their surplus employees.

2. Agency Special Selection Priority under the CTAP - Agencies must give selection priority to their own well-qualified surplus employees who apply for vacancies in other agency components in the local commuting area. Agencies must notify their surplus or displaced employees when they plan to fill these jobs. With a few exceptions, the agency must select those who apply and are eligible and well qualified before any other candidate from within or outside the agency.

3. Agency Reemployment Priority Lists (RPL) - Each agency must also maintain a Reemployment Priority List (RPL) for each local commuting area where it separates employees by reduction in force. Employees can register for the RPL to tell their former agency that they want to return if the agency has vacancies. Employees can register for their agency's RPL as soon as they receive a Reduction in Force (RIF) separation notice. Before the agency can select a candidate outside its workforce, it must first check the RPL for that location. With a few exceptions, the agency must select a qualified employee from the RPL before hiring anyone from outside the agency.

Displaced federal workers also receive priority for jobs in agencies outside the one they worked in before involuntary separation. This is done through an Interagency Career Transition Assistance Plan (ICTAP). ICTAP employees must apply for positions in the local commuting area and include proof that they were displaced. ICTAP gives an eligible, well qualified employee selection priority over almost any other applicant from outside the agency. Under ICTAP, for example, a Department of Agriculture employee with a RIF separation notice could apply for a competitive service vacancy in the local commuting area at the Department of Homeland Security. In most cases, Homeland Security must select this well qualified person for the position before choosing another applicant from outside the agency.

Veterans

Since the time of the Civil War, veterans of the Armed Forces have been given some degree of preference in appointments to federal jobs. Recognizing their sacrifice, Congress enacted laws to prevent veterans seeking federal employment from being penalized for their time in military service. Veterans' preference recognizes the economic loss suffered by citizens who have served their country in uniform, restores veterans to a favorable competitive position for government employment, and acknowledges the larger obligation owed to disabled veterans. The Department of Defense hires veterans for civilian positions at the highest rate of any federal civilian employer, frequently because veterans are prepared to stay with the government as an employer. Hiring veterans is a win/win situation: veterans will find, in the words of Senator John McCain (Arizona), "the jobs of a lifetime." With veterans appointing authorities, agencies can quickly hire people with talent. Transitioning veterans are ready to supply the very skills the federal government needs. This talent pool can be a particularly effective match with agencies needing to fill technology based positions and those helping to defend the homeland. Besides the discipline and work ethic that military service instills, transitioning veterans have technical skills in areas of critical importance: computers, communications, security, information gathering, and medical technology. Many already hold required security clearances for some federal positions.[79]

There are three ways veterans can be appointed to jobs in the competitive civil service:

- All Sources Competitive Examination appointment through an OPM list of eligibles (or agency equivalent),
- Noncompetitive appointment under special authorities that provide for conversion to the Competitive Service, or
- Merit Promotion under the Veterans Employment Opportunities Act (VEOA).

Veterans Preference

An All Sources Competitive Appointment is one in which the veteran competes with others on a certificate of eligibles. This is the normal entry route into the civil service for most employees. Veterans' preference applies in this situation, and those veterans who qualify as preference eligibles and are entitled to veterans' preference have 5 or 10 extra points added to their passing score on a civil service examination. Veterans' preference is not so much a reward for being in uniform as it is a way to help make up for the economic loss suffered by those who answered the nation's call to arms. Historically, Congress has reserved preference for those either who were disabled or who served in combat areas.

---

[79]http://www.opm.gov/Strategic_Management_of_Human_Capital/fhfrc/FLX02010.asp

Eligible veterans receive many advantages in federal employment, including preference for initial employment and a higher retention standing in the event of layoffs. However, the veterans' preference laws do not guarantee the veteran a job, nor do they give veterans preference in internal agency actions such as Merit Promotion, transfer, reassignment, and reinstatement.

Veterans' preference in its present form comes from the Veterans' Preference Act of 1944, as amended, and is now codified (law) in various provisions of title 5, United States Code. By law, veterans who are disabled or who served on active duty in the Armed Forces during certain specified time periods or in military campaigns are entitled to preference over others in hiring from All Sources Competitive Examination certificates and also in retention during reductions in force (RIF). Preference applies in hiring for virtually all jobs, whether in the competitive or Excepted Service. In addition to receiving preference in All Sources Competitive Examination appointments, veterans may be considered for special noncompetitive appointments for which only they are eligible.

To receive preference, a veteran must have been discharged or released from active duty in the Armed Forces under honorable conditions, i.e., with an honorable or general discharge. Preference applies in hiring from All Sources Competitive Examinations conducted by OPM and agencies under delegated examining authority, for most Excepted Service jobs including, Veterans Recruitment Appointments (VRA), and when agencies make temporary, term, and overseas limited appointments. Veterans' preference does not apply to promotion, reassignment, change to lower grade, transfer, or reinstatement.

Veterans' preference does not require an agency to use any particular appointment process. Agencies have broad authority under law to hire from any appropriate source of eligibles including special appointing authorities. An agency may consider candidates already in the civil service from an agency developed Merit Promotion certificate or it may reassign a current employee, transfer an employee from another agency, or reinstate a former federal employee. In addition, agencies are required to give priority consideration to displaced employees (CTAP, ICTAP).[80]

Veterans' preference gives special consideration to eligible veterans and spouses and mothers of deceased or disabled veterans looking for federal employment. Veterans who are disabled or who served on active duty in the Armed Forces during certain specified time periods or in military campaigns arc entitled to preference over nonveterans, both in hiring into the federal civil service and in retention during reductions in force. There are two classes of preference: five point and ten point.[81]

Five-point preference is given to those honorably separated veterans (this means an honorable or general discharge) who served on active duty (not active duty for training) in the Armed Forces:

---

[80] http://www.opm.gov/veterans/html/vetguide.asp#2
[81] http://www.opm.gov/Strategic_Management_of_Human_Capital/fhfrc/FLX02040.asp

- During a war;
- During the Gulf War from August 2, 1990, through January 2, 1992;
- For more than 180 consecutive days, other than for training, any part of which occurred after January 31, 1955, and before October 15, 1976;
- During the period April 28, 1952, through July 1, 1955; or
- In a campaign or expedition for which a campaign medal has been authorized, such as El Salvador, Lebanon, Grenada, Panama, Southwest Asia, Somalia, and Haiti.

Medal holders and Gulf War veterans who originally enlisted after September 7, 1980, or began active duty on or after October 14, 1982, without having previously completed 24 months of continuous active duty, must have served continuously for 24 months or the full period called or ordered to active duty. Military retirees at or above the rank of major (or equivalent) are not entitled to preference unless they are disabled veterans.

Ten-point preference is given to those honorably separated veterans who:

- Served on active duty in the Armed Forces at any time and have a present service connected disability or are receiving compensation, disability retirement benefits, or pension from the military or the Department of Veterans Affairs;
- Purple Heart recipients;
- Spouses of a veterans unable to work because of a service connected disability;
- Unmarried widows or widowers of certain deceased veterans; and
- Mothers of veterans who died in service or who became permanently and totally disabled, and who meets all conditions listed in 5 U.S.C. 2108.

Veterans Employment Opportunities Act (VEOA)

This law gives veterans access to federal job opportunities that might otherwise be closed to them. The law requires that: Agencies allow eligible veterans to compete for vacancies advertised under the agency's Merit Promotion procedures when the agency is seeking applications from individuals outside its own workforce. Every Merit Promotion Vacancy Announcement open to applicants outside an agency's workforce include a statement that these eligible veterans may apply.

A Merit Promotion selection under the VEOA is one in which the veteran competes with current federal employees through an agency's Merit Promotion Vacancy Announcement. The VEOA allows eligible veterans to apply for Merit Promotion Vacancy Announcements only if the vacancy announcement is open to candidates outside the agency.

However, agencies do not apply veterans' preference (points) when considering individuals under Merit Promotion procedures or under the VEOA. Use of this special authority, as with other authorities, is discretionary with the agency. A VEOA eligible who competes under Merit Promotion procedures and is selected will be given a career or career conditional appointment.

In order to maximize their opportunities, veterans who are eligible for both preference and noncompetitive appointment should, where possible, make sure they are being considered both competitively through an All Sources examination and noncompetitively under special authority such as the VRA.

Veterans' Recruitment Appointment (VRA)
(Formerly, Veterans' Readjustment Appointment)

A noncompetitive appointment under this special authority is one such as the Veterans Recruitment Appointment authority, formerly known as the Veterans Readjustment Appointment authority, and the special authority for 30 percent or more disabled veterans. Eligibility under these special authorities gives veterans a very significant advantage over others seeking to enter the federal service in they do not compete with them. An agency that wants to hire under one of these authorities can simply appoint the eligible veteran to any position for which the veteran is qualified. There is no red tape or special appointment procedures. However, use of these special authorities is discretionary with the agency. Veterans' preference applies when making appointments under these special authorities if there are two or more candidates and one or more is a preference eligible. These authorities provide for noncompetitive conversion to the Competitive Service after a suitable period of satisfactory service.

VRA allows appointment of eligible veterans up to the GS 11 or equivalent. Veterans are hired under excepted appointments to positions that are otherwise in the Competitive Service. After the individual satisfactorily completes two years of service, the veteran must be converted noncompetitively to a career or career conditional appointment. VRA can be a good tool for filling entry level to middle level positions. VRA eligibility applies to the following categories:

- Disabled veterans; Veterans who served on active duty in the Armed Forces during a war declared by Congress, or in a campaign or expedition for which a campaign badge has been authorized;
- Veterans who, while serving on active duty in the Armed Forces, participated in a military operation for which the Armed Forces Service Medal was awarded; and
- Veterans separated from active duty within three years.

Benefits to the hiring officials: VRA allows a manager to fill positions quickly by appointing eligible veterans to positions for which they are qualified, up to and including GS 11 or equivalent, without issuing a vacancy announcement.

30 Percent or More Disabled Veterans

This authority enables a hiring official to appoint an eligible candidate to any position for which he or she is qualified, without competition. Unlike the VRA, there is no grade level limitation. Initial appointments are time limited, lasting more than 60 days; however, the individual can be noncompetitively converted to permanent status at any time during the time-limited appointment. This authority is a good tool for filling positions at any grade level quickly. Eligibility applies to the following categories:

- Disabled veterans who were retired from active military service with a disability rating of 30 percent or more; and
- Disabled veterans rated by the Department of Veterans Affairs within the preceding year as having a compensable service connected disability of 30 percent or more.

A 30 percent or more disabled veteran appointment is an effective way to quickly appoint eligible disabled veterans to any position for which they are qualified without issuing a vacancy announcement.[82]

Reemployed Annuitant Programs

A reemployed annuitant is someone that has retired from the federal government with a CSRS or FERS pension and he or she begins employment again with the federal government. Without a special exemption, reemployed annuitants would be heavily penalized in the form of a substantial salary offset.

The federal government has recently expanded the number of agencies that may use the special exemptions to the salary offset. This enables the reemployed annuitants to receive their pension and new salary without penalty. However, under these special exemptions the reemployed annuitants are Excepted Service employees and do not receive new benefits, e.g., retirement credit, health insurance, and life insurance. Approval for these programs are usually time limited (renewed by Congress every few years) and reemployed annuitants are subject to be terminated with very little notice. CBP and FLETC are two agencies that have used these programs extensively to help in the critical shortages of key law enforcement instructor personnel.

---

[82] http://www.opm.gov/Strategic_Management_of_Human_Capital/fhfrc/FLX02020.asp

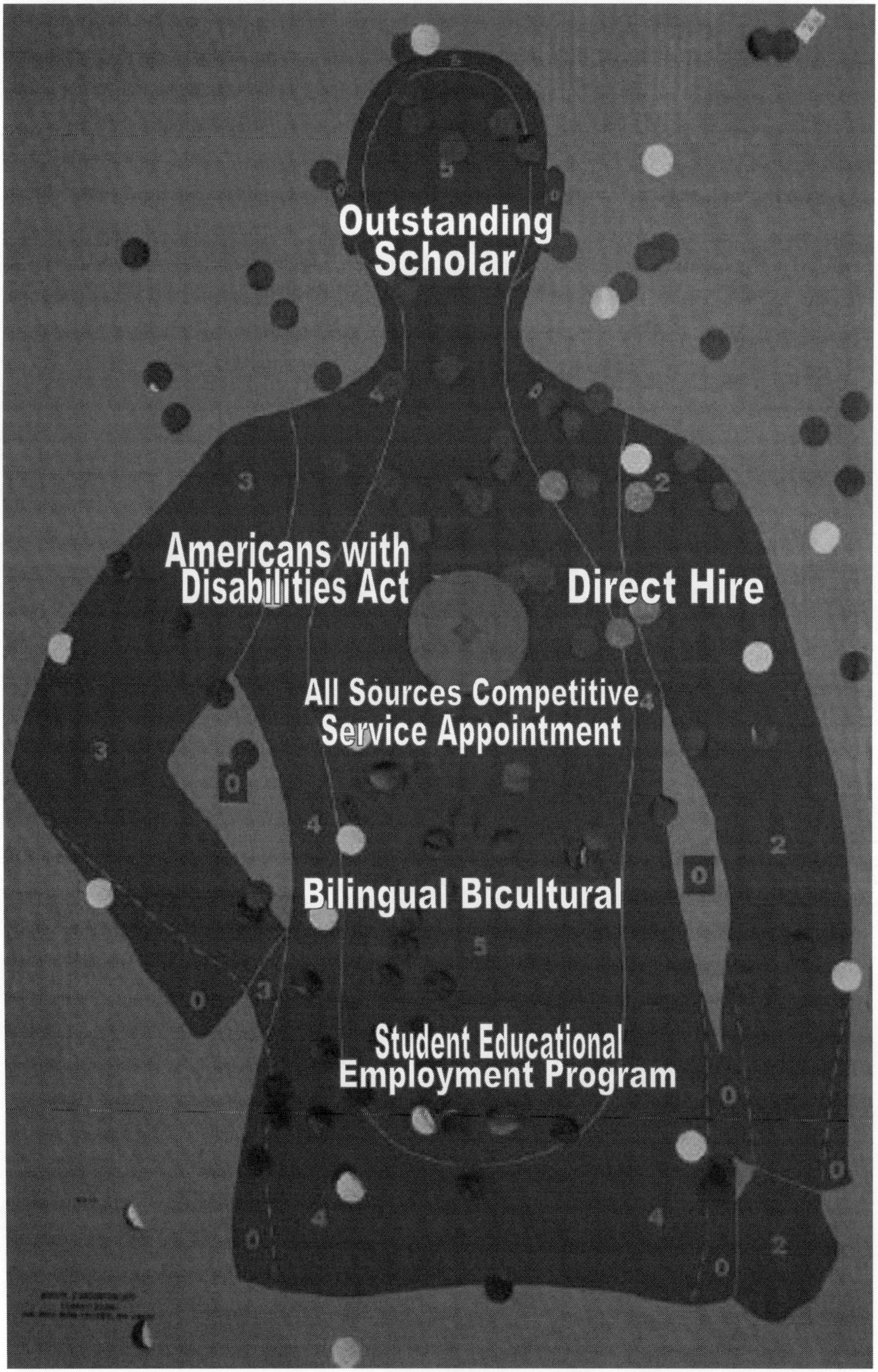
Outstanding
Scholar
Americans with
Disabilities Act
Direct Hire
All Sources Competitive
Service Appointment
Bilingual Bicultural
Student Educational
Employment Program

Outstanding Scholar Program

For informational purposes, I have included content on the Outstanding Scholar Program and the Bilingual/Bicultural Program even though OPM has directed agencies to stop using these programs. There may be an agency that chooses to ignore the OPM recommendations or is unaware of their guidance.

In a memorandum, OPM stated, Agencies are no longer required to use the Outstanding Scholar program or the Bilingual/Bicultural hiring authority, under any circumstances. The circumstances under which the consent decree did require use of these authorities are no longer applicable. Accordingly, the consent decree no longer mandates use of the Outstanding Scholar and Bilingual/Bicultural hiring authorities. In light of a recent decision by the Merit Systems Protection Board, OPM strongly advises against further use of the Outstanding Scholar and Bilingual/Bicultural hiring authorities. In October 2006, in Dean v. Department of Agriculture and Olson v. Department of Veterans Affairs, the MSPB determined it is unlawful to use the Outstanding Scholar hiring authority (and, by implication, the Bilingual/Bicultural authority) without applying veterans' preference. It does not appear possible for agencies to use the Outstanding Scholar or the Bilingual/Bicultural hiring authorities and comply with the veterans' preference provisions in title 5 as the MSPB now requires. Accordingly, OPM believes that agencies should discontinue their use of these special hiring authorities. OPM has conferred with the Department of Justice and DOJ concurs with these recommendations.[83]

Americans with Disabilities Act

The Americans with Disabilities Act (ADA) does provide a hiring authority for federal agencies to hire persons with severe disabilities. Unfortunately, the current regulation that provides Excepted Service employment opportunities for the disabled recognizes only severe disabilities. Most persons with severe disabilities are unable to perform the bona fide job requirements of a law enforcement officer and therefore would be ineligible for the position. Exceptions to this likely includes persons with an amputation who can perform the requisite job functions like running, or shooting a pistol with either hand.

Officially, applicants with disabilities must have mental retardation, a severe physical disability or a psychiatric disability; have proof of the disability; certification of job readiness (if not hired on a temporary appointment in lieu of the job readiness certification); and meet all required qualifications for the position. For information on specific application steps and more information on this topic go to: http://www.opm.gov/disability/appointment_disabilities.asp

---

[83] http://www.opm.gov/employ/luevano-archive.asp

Using OPM approved government wide or agency specific direct hire authorities, agencies may appoint candidates directly to jobs, without regard to the provisions title 5 U.S.C. 3309 through 3318, for which OPM determines there is a severe shortage of candidates or critical hiring need. Direct hire authority is commonly used to hire medical professionals; however, we may see agencies use direct hire authority in law enforcement jobs after a major crisis such as September 11, 2001, or hurricane Katrina. When using the direct hire authorities, agencies must adhere to public notice requirements and displaced employee procedures (ICTAP).[84] Although the term "direct hire" is used, the authority essentially provides for a noncompetitive appointment to the Competitive Service. "Direct hire" means the ability to hire without having to assess candidates, but only when there are less than four candidates and there are no candidates eligible for veterans' preference. The Outstanding Scholar program did not have that restriction. Rating and ranking are not required, so neither the "rule of three" nor veterans' preference are applied. There are requirements, however, the positions be announced, that displaced employees be given preference, and the program only be used as a supplement to competitive examining.

All Sources Competitive Examination

The All Sources Competitive Examination hiring authority is open to all applicants (All Sources) the process can be used by:

- candidates who apply from outside the federal workforce,
- current federal employees without career or career conditional status to compete for a permanent appointment, and
- employees with career or career conditional status to compete for other federal positions.

The All Sources Competitive Examination method is the most often used hiring authority to fill entry-level law enforcement jobs in the Competitive Service. This process uses quantifiable ratings to determine who is highly qualified for the job. To ensure that selections are made from among the best-qualified available candidates the government will compare applicant's qualifications to job related criteria as measured by valid selection devices. Among the variety of devices that are used to examine applicants qualifications, the two most common are:

1. Written Tests (also called assembled examinations because applicants assemble in one place and time and take the same exam...kind of like the SAT).

---

[84] http://www.opm.gov/employ/html/sroa2.asp

2. Evaluation of Experience (also called unassembled examinations. An unassembled examination is an assessment and rating of the applicant's education and experience against job related knowledge, skills, and abilities. There is no need for the applicants to gather together.)

The All Sources Competitive Examination rules are probably the single largest contributing source for frustration and discontent in the federal hiring process. Enter stage right: the "rule of three" and "veterans' Passover rules." The rule of three and veterans Passover rules make it very difficult for selecting officials to select nonveterans that apply for an All Sources Vacancy Announcement. In fact, this difficulty has given rise to new terminology: It is said that someone "blocks the list" when there is a situation where the rule of three prevents the selecting official from picking their preferred applicant. Blocking the list simply means a person lower on the list could not be reached.

These rules require that selection from a certificate of eligible applicants be made from the highest three eligibles on the list who are available for the job, the rule of three. However, an agency may not pass over a preference eligible to select a lower ranking nonpreference eligible or nonpreference eligible with the same or lower score. A preference eligible means an applicant with a 5 or 10-point veterans' preference score. A nonpreference eligible means an applicant that does not qualify for the 5 or 10 point veterans' preference points. Example: If the top person on a certificate is a 10-point disabled veteran and the second and third persons are 5-point preference eligibles, the hiring officials may choose any of the three. If the top person on a certificate is a 10 point disabled veteran, the second person is a nonpreference eligible, and the third person is a 5-point preference eligible, the selecting official may choose either of the preference eligibles. The hiring officials may not pass over the 10 point disabled veteran to select the nonpreference eligible unless the preference eligible is disqualified or withdraws his name from consideration. Keep in mind; these rules apply to All Sources Competitive Examination certificates and not Merit Promotion certificates.

Disqualifications of preference eligibles can occur but require a lot of documentation and work on the agency's part. An agency that is trying to work the list to reach an applicant they really want sometimes will telephone applicants on the list to inquire if they are still interested in the position. In a twist on the rule of three, an appointing official is not required to consider a person who has three times been passed over with appropriate approval or who has already been considered for three separate appointments from the same or different certificates for the same position. However, in each of these considerations, the person must have been within reach under the rule of three and a selection must have been made from that group of three. Further, the preference eligible is entitled to advance notice of discontinuance of certification.[85]

---

[85]http://www.opm.gov/veterans/html/vetguide.asp

The bottom line is that if you are a preference eligible, the odds are stacked in your favor and you should use the All Sources Competitive Examination hiring authority to your advantage. If you are a not a veteran or a veteran without preference points, understand that you will have a difficult time beating out preference eligibles on an All Sources Competitive Examination. I encourage you to apply for the All Sources Vacancy Announcement you desire but do not be disappointed if you never get the phone call asking: "When can you start?" Those without preference points may want to focus their attention on other hiring authorities like Merit Promotion or internships.

Future of Hiring Authorities

It is worth noting that hiring authorities change over time. Be prepared to take advantage of the dynamic hiring authorities. Just as Outstanding Scholar and Bilingual/Bicultural programs have been put on hold, others are starting fresh. Those who listened closely to President Bush's 2008 State of the Union Address may have heard the foreshadowing of a new hiring authority. He said, "Our military families also sacrifice for America. They endure sleepless nights and the daily struggle of providing for children while a loved one is serving far from home. We have a responsibility to provide for them. Therefore, I ask you to join me in expanding their access to childcare, **creating new hiring preferences for military spouses across the federal government**, and allowing our troops to transfer their unused education benefits to their spouses or children. Our military families serve our nation, they inspire our nation, and tonight our nation honors them."

Internships

When most people think of internships they have thoughts of very limited pay and entry requirements designed specifically for students. While this is true for some federal internship programs, it does not hold true for all. Typically, the guiding thrust behind an agency's internship program is to identify and recruit the best and brightest to their organization. Some government internships also focus on helping certain groups such as students with disabilities or students that are economically disadvantaged. Many of the federal internships offer pay or per diem (compensation for food and housing) while some are strictly voluntary.

For the programs that offer minimal compensation, my experience is that students conditioned to the typical college life will likely see any pay or per diem as a windfall. It is all about perspective; studies have shown that persons who are able to delay gratification for future rewards will be well ahead of the game in the end when compared to those who require immediate payoff. Why should someone seek an internship position? Simply put, it is another legitimate method to get to the result, a federal law enforcement job.

The Federal Career Intern Program (FCIP) and the two programs of the Student Educational Employment Program (SEEP) are excellent methods to get into law enforcement careers. These programs may allow interns noncompetitive conversion to full-time equivalent Competitive Service positions. There are a few good reasons why everyone, not just young adults, should apply for internships. The most important reason is the FCIP does not stipulate the intern be enrolled in school. By design, non-students should apply for FCIP internships.

In contrast, SEEP internships are specifically designed for students; however, there are no maximum age requirements. The SEEP programs create a nice loophole for anyone having difficulty getting a federal law enforcement job through competitive hiring authorities. Web based educational opportunities mitigate the most common excuses for older adults not going to college. The Chapter that follows, Internships, provides information on specific agency Internships while the information that follows immediately highlights important attributes of various intern programs.

The FCIP is not what I think of when envisioning an internship. In fact, I do not see any differences in the FCIP and the All Sources Competitive hiring authority other than the Excepted Service probationary period. Officially, the FCIP program is a comprehensive two-year entry-level employment and career development program. The purpose of the Program is to attract exceptional men and women to the federal workforce who have diverse professional experiences, academic training, and competencies, and to prepare them for careers in analyzing and implementing public programs.

"Career Intern" is a generic term, and agencies may use occupational titles as appropriate. It was created under Executive Order 13162, and is intended for positions at grade levels GS 5, 7, and 9. In general, individuals are appointed to a two-year internship. Upon successful completion of the internships, the interns may be eligible for permanent placement within an agency. Individuals interested in Career Intern opportunities must contact specific agencies directly. OPM is not the central source for career intern opportunities.[86] President William J. Clinton signed the executive order on July 6, 2000, and it states:

OPM shall develop appropriate merit based procedures for the recruitment, screening, placement, and continuing career development of Career Interns. In developing those procedures, OPM shall provide for such actions as deemed appropriate to assure equal employment opportunity and the application of appropriate veterans' preference criteria. A successful candidate shall be appointed to a position in Schedule B of the Excepted Service at the GS 5, 7, or 9 (and equivalent) or other trainee level appropriate for the Program, unless otherwise approved by OPM. The appointment shall not exceed two years unless extended by the federal department or agency, with the concurrence of OPM, for up to one additional year.

Except as provided; service, as a Career Intern confers no rights to further federal employment in either the competitive or Excepted Service upon the expiration of the internship period.

- Competitive civil service status may be granted to a Career Intern who satisfactorily completes the internship and meets all other requirements prescribed by OPM.
- Within an agency, an employee who formerly held a career or career conditional appointment immediately before entering the Career Intern Program, and who fails to complete the Career Intern Program for reasons unrelated to misconduct or suitability, shall be placed in a career or career conditional position in the current agency at no lower grade or pay than the one the employee left to accept the position in the Career Intern Program.[87]

In contrast to the FCIP, there is the SEEP, which is comprised of two internship programs and provides federal employment opportunities to students. A student is defined as an individual enrolled or accepted for enrollment as a degree seeking student (diploma, certificate) taking at least a half-time academic, vocational or technical course load in an accredited high school, technical or vocational, college or university, graduate or professional school.

---

[86]http://www.opm.gov/careerintern/
[87]http://www.opm.gov/EO/13162.asp

The SEEP programs were established December 16, 1994, in an effort to streamline, replace, and consolidate four older federal student employment programs: Cooperative Education Program, Federal Junior Fellowship Program, Stay-In-School Program, and Harry S. Truman Scholarship Program. The new streamlined program is comprised of two components, the Student Temporary Employment Program (STEP) and the Student Career Experience Program (SCEP). Both components are available to all levels of students: high school, vocational and technical, associate degree, baccalaureate degree, graduate degree, and professional degree students. Thus, under the SEEP Programs, a federal agency may hire students as temporary employees or as permanent, career employees. Participants of either program are appointed to the Excepted Service and they can be noncompetitively converted to the Competitive Service.

The STEP provides for maximum flexibility to both students and agencies by offering valuable temporary work experiences. The STEP allows a student to work in a professional, administrative, technical, clerical, or trades/labor position with duties that do not have to be directly related to the student's academic field of study and career goals. However, a STEP participant may, at a later time, be noncompetitively converted to the SCEP Program and perform work tasks related to his or her academic field of study.

The SCEP provides for long term, committed, career track work experience, which must be directly related to the student's academic field of study and career goals. Participants of the SCEP may be noncompetitively converted to term, career-conditional, or career appointments following the successful completion of all academic and work experience requirements within a certain time limitation. The SCEP is designed to combine classroom learning with practical on-the-job experience. It enables the student to apply the theory and skills learned in the classroom to the on-the-job training.

The SEEP enables an agency and supervisor to recognize and evaluate first-hand the abilities of a potential student employee, and their performance in real work situations. In addition, the SEEP allows for continuing recruitment and development of potential and talented student employees to support changing agency missions; ensure the government can meet its professional, technical, and administrative needs; and achieve a quality and diverse workforce.

The benefits of the SEEP and its components are as follows:

- Exposure to professional agency work experience that may be directly and/or indirectly related to a student's academic field of study and/or career goals;
- Opportunity for career development and training;
- Formal mentoring program;
- Competitive salary based upon education and related work experience;
- STEP participant - may earn vacation and sick leave, and holiday pay only;
- SCEP participant - may earn vacation and sick leave; holiday pay; and also eligible for health and life insurance, and retirements benefits;
- SCEP participant - eligible for travel assistance to and from the work site, if more than 100 miles round trip from the work site;
- SCEP participant - eligible for tuition assistance;
- SCEP participant - eligible for rapid promotion.[88]

What are the differences between the STEP and SCEP? Students hired under the STEP authority are not eligible for noncompetitive conversion into permanent, full-time equivalent positions. Students hired under the SCEP authority may be noncompetitively converted to term, career, or career conditional appointments following completion of their academic and work experience requirements.

How does a student transition from being in the STEP or SCEP to being a permanent employee? (Note: Noncompetitive conversion to a FTE position requires the student attain SCEP status before graduation.) A student is required to work 640 hours, without a break in service, prior to being converted to a permanent position. The most common manner in which this is done is for a student to be hired into the STEP and sometime before graduation, be converted to the SCEP. Provided the relationship between the student and the agency is acceptable, and depending on whether the student is a freshman, sophomore, junior, or senior, the student may terminate his employment with the agency at the end of the summer and return to school.

Students hired via the SCEP authority, may be placed on non-pay status at the end of the summer to ensure the time in service is not broken and the 640 hours are earned prior to conversion to a permanent position. Agency student employment coordinators are urged to try to place the graduates with other agencies, if placement in their own agency is not possible.[89]

---

[88]http://www.nv.blm.gov/seep_external/documents/student_educ_emply_prog/seep.htm
[89]http://www.blm.gov/cadastral/Manual/pdffiles/FrequentlyAskedQuestions2007.pdf

Chapter 7: Internships

Federal internships are not just for college students. Case in point is the FCIP. It is specifically designed to reach persons outside of academia. Persons seeking federal employment must consider internships as a method of getting a law enforcement job or they may never achieve their goal. In the case of the FCIP, calling it a mentoring program would be more descriptive than an internship program. With SEEP programs, persons not enrolled in the applicable educational school can change their status by becoming students no matter what age. This chapter focuses on specific agency internships as opposed to the internship section within the previous chapter, which provides an overview of the major types of intern hiring authorities.

Border Patrol FCIP Internships

I believe the Border Patrol FCIP offers the single greatest opportunity for those persons having difficulty getting into federal law enforcement. What types of positions are being filled? Border Patrol Agent positions are full-time positions filled under the FCIP. The FCIP is a program that helps federal agencies recruit talented individuals for entry-level government positions. FCIP appointments are designed with a two-year internship, during which time you will be learning the job and the organization, attending formal training programs and developing your skills. If your performance and conduct are satisfactory, your appointment will be made permanent after the two-year internship. The Federal Career Intern Program is an Excepted Service appointing authority.

Starting Salary and Career Progression - As a Border Patrol Agent, entry level is either at grade GL 5 or GL 7, depending on qualifications. You can advance from a GL 5 entry-level position through GL 9 and up to the GS 11 full performance level without having to reapply. Generally, Border Patrol Agents receive these promotions after performing satisfactorily for one year at each grade level. The Border Patrol Agent position has an accelerated promotion plan, which means that upon successful completion of the 6 1/2 month probationary examination, individuals hired at the GL 5 level are eligible for promotion to the GL 7, and individuals hired at the GL 7 are eligible for promotion to GL 9.

Step 1 Apply by Internet - You must register for the written test for the Border Patrol Agent position during the open period. You must register for the written test online through the Internet at https://cbpmhc.hr-services.org/Border Patrol Agent/ . The Web site address is available 24 hours per day, 7 days a week during the open period. Based on your responses to the questions, OPM will determine if you meet the basic qualifications for the Border Patrol Agent position. If you appear to meet the minimum qualifications, you will be scheduled for the written test.

Step 2 Written Test - Scheduling of the written test is done during the online registration process. As soon as you have registered and been scheduled for the written test, you will be able to print your test admission notice which will contain the date, location, and time for the written test. This admission notice will also include the contact information for OPM. If you are unable to print your test admission notice, instructions will be provided online for requesting that a copy be mailed to you. If you are unable to attend your scheduled test date and you are unable to reschedule your test date with OPM, you will need to wait for the next Border Patrol Agent open period and re-register.

For those who register to take the written test at a compressed testing location, CBP will be utilizing a special process that requires approximately 8 hours of your time on the day of the test. Compressed testing will be conducted in Tucson, Arizona; Moreno Valley, California; Holtville, California; San Diego, California; Denver, Colorado; Orlando, Florida; Atlanta, Georgia; Buffalo, New York; New York, New York; San Antonio, Texas; El Paso, Texas; McAllen, Texas; Chicago, Illinois; Detroit, Michigan; Dallas, Texas; Houston, Texas; Phoenix, Arizona and Bellevue, Washington. The initial step in the process is the test itself. After completing the test, a Border Patrol Agent will present an orientation session about the position. You will be given a copy of your test results (Notice of Results). If you successfully pass the written exam, you will be given a packet of forms to complete and mail to the Minneapolis Hiring Center as well as a date (within four weeks of the examination) for an Oral Board Interview.

Step 3 Selection Process - For those who register to take the written test at an expedited testing location, CBP will also be utilizing the same process that requires 8 hours of your time on the first day and includes an orientation session with a Border Patrol Agent. However, if you successfully pass the test, you will be given the time, date and location of when you are required to return to complete your fitness/medical tests and oral board interview, which is approximately 31 days from the date you took your written test. If you pass the written test, your name will be placed in an inventory. The inventory is maintained in test score order (highest to lowest).

Nationwide Testing - Selection from the Nationwide Testing process is done once a month. Approximately two weeks after you take the written test you will receive your Notice of Results (NOR) in the mail informing you of whether or not you passed the written test. If you successfully pass the test, you will receive a tentative selection packet about six weeks from the date you passed your written test. After you receive your tentative selection packet, you will be scheduled for your fitness/medical tests and oral board interview. This usually takes place within four weeks of receiving your tentative selection packet.

Compressed Testing - Selection from the Compressed Testing process is done every two weeks. You will be given your NOR the same day that you take the written exam. If you successfully pass the written exam, you will be given a tentative selection packet at that time and scheduled for an oral board interview. Within four weeks, you will be scheduled for your medical and fitness tests.

Expedited Testing - Selection from the Expedited Testing process is done every two weeks. You will be given your NOR the same day that you take the written exam. If you successfully pass the written exam, you will be given a tentative selection packet at that time and informed of when you will be required to return to complete your fitness/medical tests and oral board interview, which is approximately 31 days from the date you took your written test. The tentative selection packet contains information that you will need to submit to the Minneapolis Hiring Center by the required date and includes instructions on how to complete each form. The packet includes information about the oral board interview, fitness/medical tests, vision requirements, drug testing, and the background investigation.

Step 4-Structured Oral Interview - The Oral Board is a structured interview given by three Border Patrol Agents. The interview consists of situational questions that do not require technical knowledge. The structured interview assesses a candidate's judgment/decision making, emotional maturity, interpersonal skills, and cooperativeness/sensitivity to the needs of others. These qualities are key to successful performance as a Border Patrol Agent. The oral board is a pass/fail interview. Candidates must receive a "pass" in all areas in order to continue in the hiring process. The Oral Board Interview usually takes place within four to six weeks after you receive a tentative selection letter. The scheduling of the interview will depend on the type of testing process you chose. If you are in the expedited process, you will need to come back in 31 days to take the interview. If you took the compressed test, you will be scheduled for the interview within four to six weeks of your written test date.

Step 5 Preemployment Process - In addition to completing step 4, you must also undergo and successfully complete a drug test, medical examination, and fitness exam and background investigation. These will be scheduled and completed as soon as possible. After completing all these steps, sit back, relax, and wait for the phone call offering you the job. On the other hand, you may want to try the Marshals Service Internship to increase your odds of success.

Marshals Service FCIP Internships

The FCIP gives the Marshals Service greater flexibility in recruiting, assessing and selecting candidates to fill Deputy Marshal Positions. FCIP is a formal training and development program that can be used to attract high potential individuals to the federal government, specifically with the Marshals Service. There will no longer be a written test requirement for the Deputy position under FCIP. Individuals are hired for two-year internships in the Excepted Service and may be converted to permanent appointments in the Competitive Service upon completing the program and meeting all qualifications, suitability and performance requirements. Individuals selected will fill entry-level Deputy positions, GS 082, at the GS 5 or GS 7 level.

The Marshals Service will continue to use the more traditional methods that have in the past proven effective in attracting and retaining high quality candidates. These include Centralized Student Career Experience Program (CSCEP), internal Merit Promotion, lateral candidates, reinstatement of former Deputies, and Merit Promotion. The Executive order establishing FCIP does not exempt agencies from the Veterans Preference Act of 1944, as amended, or from applying part 302 procedures. Deputy applicants will be placed in quality groupings and veterans' preference points will be added. Compensable vets will be at the top of their respective quality groups.

Applicants who meet the necessary qualifications are required to successfully complete a structured interview and a writing sample exercise. Those who are made a conditional offer of employment must successfully complete a full field background investigation, medical examination, drug test, FIT assessment and a final review by a panel of senior operational Marshals Service employees. Deputy Interns are in a trial period for the entire period of internship. During this trial period, they will be regularly counseled and evaluated on their performance. Continuation of the program is contingent upon satisfactory performance during the internship period.

In accordance with the regulations for FCIP, all selected Deputy Interns will have a focused training plan. The plan begins with attending initial Deputy training at the Marshals Service Federal Law Enforcement Training Center in Glynco, GA. This initial training will be a 17 1/2 week comprehensive curriculum, which includes the Criminal Investigator Training Program. Training and development activities will continue to be the focus of the FCIP as Deputy Interns complete the first two years of the three year Deputy Development Program.

Deputy Interns will not be required to serve a probationary period following their conversion to the Competitive Service. The two years the employees spend on the excepted appointment will serve as the employee's trial period. A Deputy Intern may be promoted to the next higher level if they meet all the agency qualifications and eligibility requirements necessary for promotion and have successfully completed applicable training requirements. The Deputy Intern may be converted to a permanent appointment in the Competitive Service upon completing the program and meeting all qualifications, suitability and performance requirements. This noncompetitive conversion to the

Competitive Service will be effective on the date the two-year service requirement is met. If a Deputy Intern is not performing at the Successful level, at any time, he or she may be removed from the Program.

The Marshals Service has begun its initial use of FCIP in several large metropolitan areas and some non-continental United States districts. These districts have FCIP Recruiting Officers who have begun a recruitment program with outreach to colleges, law enforcement organizations, and military transition bases. The following Marshals Service districts are participating in the initial group: DC/SC, C/CA, N/CA, S/NY, S/TX, W/TX, D/VI, D/PR, S/FL, D/GU, D/AZ, and D/NM.

Applicants must meet the minimum qualifications to be a Deputy Marshal. These qualifications can be found on the Marshals Service Public Web site. For more information, an applicant should contact a FCIP Recruiting Officer in a participating district. An applicant must attend an Informational Session Seminar hosted by the participating district. These seminars are offered on a limited basis during the year. At the seminar, applicants will be given specific instruction regarding the application process. It is up to the applicant to provide current contact information to the FCIP Recruiters and ensure the information is updated if any changes occur.[90]

The NCIS Student Educational Employment Program (SEEP)

The NCIS SEEP is a dedicated hands-on experience designed to provide educationally related work assignments for students in a nonpaid status. Based upon their background and experience, interns are assigned to functional areas such as criminal investigations, information systems, government relations and public affairs, administrative services, computer crimes, economic crimes, strategic planning, personnel services and operations, criminal intelligence, and forensic sciences.

NCIS is seeking individuals who possess strong academic credentials, outstanding character, and a high degree of motivation. In order to be considered for the Program, individuals must meet the following criteria:

- Be currently enrolled not less than half time in a baccalaureate (Junior/Senior status) or graduate degree program (freshman/sophomore students may compete for specified positions in the administrative arena);
- Maintain a minimum 3.0 cumulative grade point average;[91]
- United States citizenship and
- Favorable completion of criminal history checks.

There are specific things that will automatically disqualify a student from consideration for the NCIS Student Internship Program. They are:

---

[90] http://www.usmarshals.gov/careers/fcip_faq.htm

[91] Students who do not meet the minimum GPA may apply; however, they must submit 2 STRONG letters of recommendation from professors or faculty member and should include a statement in their package explaining reasons for low grades/GPA.

- Conviction of a felony;
- Use of illegal drugs. The NCIS is firmly committed to a drug free society and workplace. Students applying for the NCIS Internship Program must be considered eligible for employment upon completion of their degree program.

FBI Internship Programs

The FBI has numerous internship opportunities available for undergraduate and graduate students seeking to contribute to the FBI's mission and learn more about what it is like to work at the FBI. Click here for a link to the FBI's Internship web page.

- Honors Internship Program
- Middle Eastern Foreign Language Honors Internship Program
- Volunteer Internship Programs
- Visiting Scientist Program
- National Security Internship

The Honors Internship and Volunteer Internship Programs are the two likely to have the most interest for those seeking law enforcement careers.

FBI Honors Internship Program

Each summer, a special group of outstanding undergraduate and graduate students are selected to participate in the FBI Honors Internship Program in Washington, D.C., or at a Regional Computer Forensics Laboratory (RCFL) located throughout the United States (www.rcfl.gov). Interested applicants should continue to view the FBI's Web site for updates and instructions on how to apply for the summer 2009 Honors Internship Program. The application deadline for the summer 2009 program is October 10, 2008.

The FBI Honors Internship Program offers undergraduate and graduate school students an exciting insider's view of FBI operations and provides an opportunity to explore the many career opportunities within the Bureau. The Honors Internship Program brings students to work at FBI Headquarters in Washington, D.C., and usually begins on the first Monday in June and ends on the second Friday in August. FBI Honors Interns can look forward to ten extremely rewarding and interesting weeks. You will be working side-by-side with Special Agents and Professional Staff personnel on important cases and management issues. You will feel like you are a part of the Bureau...because you are.

Honors Interns are assigned to an FBI Headquarters division based on their academic discipline, potential contribution to the division, and the needs of the FBI. For instance, Honors Interns whose discipline is in the physical sciences may be assigned to the FBI's Laboratory Division in nearby Quantico, Virginia. Honors Interns whose discipline is in information technology may be assigned to the FBI's Cyber Division or one of the FBI's IT divisions. All Honors Interns are under the supervision of the head (i.e., Assistant Director) of their assigned division.

By the end of your internship, you will have a thorough understanding of the inner workings of the FBI and a deep feeling of satisfaction the work you have done has helped the lives of ordinary citizens. You will also learn about the many career opportunities at the FBI. No matter what career path you eventually choose, serving as an FBI Honors Intern will be an experience you will never forget, and one that will benefit you in all of your future endeavors.

Due to the very selective and highly competitive nature of the FBI Honors Internship Program, a limited number of internships are awarded each summer. Only individuals possessing strong academic credentials, outstanding character, a high degree of motivation, and the willingness to represent the FBI upon returning to their respective campuses will be selected. In order to be considered, individuals must meet all of the following qualifications at the time they apply:

- Candidates must be attending a college or university that is accredited by one of the regional or national institutional associations recognized by the United States Secretary of Education;
- Undergraduate students must be in their junior or senior year, attending a college or university full-time;
- Graduate students must be enrolled in a college or university, attending full-time;
- All applicants must be returning to their respective schools for at least one semester immediately following the completion of the internship;
- Students must have a minimum cumulative grade point average of 3.0 or above on a 4.0 scale and be in good standing with their academic institution; and
- Candidates must be citizens of the United States, must meet all FBI Employment Requirements, be able to pass an FBI Background Investigation, and receive a Top Secret Security Clearance

Candidates must submit their completed package to the FBI field office nearest their campus by the published date. FBI representatives from each Field Office will arrange interviews with the most competitive candidates. Interviews normally take place in October. Each field office then nominates a designated number of candidates to FBI Headquarters (FBIHQ) in Washington, D.C., by early November.

A Headquarters selection committee will make the final determination of successful candidates. Selections are based upon academic achievements, area of study, life/work experiences, and the needs of the FBI. The FBI actively seeks women, minorities and persons with disabilities for participation in the Honors Internship Program. Final decisions are generally made in November of each year, and selected candidates receive a conditional job offer soon thereafter. The initial offer is conditional because candidates selected must undergo an extensive FBI Background Investigation and receive an FBI Top Secret Clearance in order to be eligible to participate in the program.

Undergraduate Honors Interns are paid at the GS 6 grade level on the government pay scale. The FBI also reimburses for some travel expenses to and from Washington, D.C., at the beginning and end of the Honors Internship program. Interns participating in a Regional Computer Forensics Laboratory (RCFL) are expected to already live within commutable distance and will not receive reimbursement for travel expenses to and from their assigned RCFL. Any travel on behalf of the RCFL or FBIHQ during the internship will be reimbursed by the FBI hiring entity.[92]

The FBI Volunteer Internship Program

The FBI Volunteer Internship Program offers high school, undergraduate, and graduate students an exciting insider's view of FBI operations and provides an opportunity to explore the many career opportunities within the Bureau.[93] Click here for a link to their Web site with the various volunteer opportunities.

FLETC Voluntary Internships

The FLETC College Intern Program provides a unique opportunity for interns to participate in the Federal law enforcement-training environment. Three sessions of the College Intern Program are conducted annually. Sessions are twelve weeks in length.

Each intern is assigned a mentor in one of the FLETC training divisions or a mentor from one of the onsite Partner Organizations. The program is designed so that, overall, half of the session is spent attending various components of federal law enforcement basic and advanced training programs, and the remaining half of the session is spent working on meaningful law enforcement training related research and writing projects under the guidance of the intern's mentor.

In addition to access to FLETC's training and recreational opportunities, interns receive $49 per session day of taxable income to help defray the cost of meals, incidental expenses, and travel costs. Interns are required to live on the FLETC facility in a dormitory at no cost. Interns are issued uniforms for training and physical conditioning, which must be worn every training day.
Students majoring or obtaining advanced degrees in Criminal Justice, Criminal Justice Administration, Forensic Sciences, Psychology, or Computer Forensics, as well as

---

[92]http://www.fbijobs.gov/231.asp
[93]http://www.fbijobs.gov/239.asp

students pursuing Juris Doctorate degrees are the norm, although students with other majors or focuses have been selected in the past. Of critical importance is the applicant's desire to pursue a career in Federal law enforcement.

- Applicants must be enrolled in either a baccalaureate or a graduate program both at the time of application and at the time, the internship will be served.
- Applicants must be a senior or graduate student. To qualify as a senior, applicants must have completed 135 quarter hours or 90 semester hours of a baccalaureate program, but not be granted a degree by the date the intern session will end.
- Applicants must be enrolled in a degree program, which has a mandatory requirement of successful completion of an internship. Every applicant must be in the upper third of his or her class in academic standing.
- Applicants must be citizens of the United States.

Selection is highly competitive, and is based upon: grade point averages, both in the applicant's major and overall; leadership and community participation; work experiences; professional experiences related to the applicant's major; the contents and communication skills reflected in the applicant's narrative essay; the contents of the submitted Intern Nomination form; and, if the applicant successfully makes it through the initial selection process, the responses given during a telephonic interview.

All requirements are mandatory and none can be waived without the approval of the intern coordinator. There will be no discrimination in qualifying, certifying, ranking or selection because of race, color, religion, sex, national origin, political affiliations, marital status, physical handicap, age, or membership or non-membership in an employee organization. Prior to official notification of selection, intern candidates will be subjected to a background investigation and records checks.

More information is available at the FLETC intern Web site by clicking here. Specific FLETC Intern Program information, Intern applications and information regarding procedures and forms may be received by contacting FLETC-Interns@dhs.gov at (912) 267-3221.

Other Internship Resources

Internships represent the single best method for persons to noncompetively get appointed to law enforcement positions. While the few agencies presented in this Chapter are representative of programs across the entire federal government, they are just a small sample. The best place for finding a broad spectrum of comprehensive contact information about federal internships is through a Web site provided by Congressman Watt. Many of the agencies listed in his Web site are not necessarily, law enforcement; however, keep in mind that a federal law enforcement agency may be able to hire you noncompetitively even if you are in a federal internship that is not law enforcement related. http://watt.house.gov/internshiplistings.asp

Chapter 8: Resumes, Applications, and Testing

Some of the most important information to know regarding the federal hiring process is the value and purpose of various documents and paperwork submitted to the agency. It is even more important to understand the methods of assessment.

Resumes

The resume for most entry-level law enforcement positions is nothing more than a starting document for the agency to gather requisite information to determine if the applicant meets the minimum qualifications. Whether the resume is submitted online or in paper form, ensure the information is accurate and without spelling and grammar errors. If you are submitting the resume in paper form, I recommend using the OF 612 form rather than the SF 171 or business resume.

Online resumes, such as the USAJobs resume builder, allow you to cut and paste from most types of digital resume documents that you may have created for previous job applications. This is a nice feature because you do not want to recreate the wheel. Be aware of the problems with cutting and pasting text; mainly that the probability of a new mistake is increased. Your masterpiece of a resume viewed on word processing software may highlight spelling and grammar errors in nice pretty colors. The Web based resume will not creatively identify these errors. Print out a hard copy of the Web based resume and have someone proof if for you.

From my view, applicants often overrate the importance of the resumes. I base this opinion on my experience that a resume only gets you to the next step, at most a seat at the interview table and not a job offer. I have seen too many people spending an inordinate amount of time writing and rewriting their resume and these same people believe if they had only written it better or used a particular buzzword they would have gotten the job. To me, the federal resume should be thought of as fitting into the "all or none rule." What I mean by this is the resume will usually fit into one of two categories. The first category is "Acceptable" the second is "Unacceptable." If we look at the resume as being the first step in the application process, your goal with the resume is to make it good enough to get invited to the second step. One of the best federal documents that I have come across regarding how to write a resume can be found at: http://www.nps.gov/training/tel/Guides/Federal_Resume_pg_20060407.pdf

Applicant Examination

The All Sources Competitive Examination hiring authority uses an applicant examination process. The process attempts to quantify (provide a numerical score to) each application. The applicant examination is vitally important to the job seeker because a list containing the names of highly qualified persons is derived from the ordinal rank of applicants' examination scores. This list is officially known as a certificate. The selecting official to pick which candidate is to be hired uses it. A number of different examining devices or methods could be used to measure the degree to which applicants possess the competencies necessary for successful job performance. The examining methods have traditionally been divided into two broad categories:

1. Assembled Examinations, and
2. Unassembled Examinations.

Technically speaking, assembled in this context simply means that applicants gather together in one location or many different locations at the same time. Assembled examinations often include written tests, fitness tests, and assessment interviews. Unassembled examinations include, work samples, KSA written narratives, and questionnaires.

Assessing an applicant's KSAs or questionnaire can obviously be done without assembling everyone together in one place, thus the name unassembled examination. Most entry-level law enforcement jobs with multiple openings use assembled examinations while most career advancement positions have traditionally used unassembled exams in the form of KSA written narratives.

Assembled Examinations

The most commonly used assessments for an assembled examination are:

- written tests,
- fitness tests, and
- assessment interviews.

Written Tests

Written tests are the number one method used for mass hiring is of persons in entry-level law enforcement positions. There are many different types of written tests. The two most familiar types are achievement tests and aptitude tests. Achievement tests measure what is already known while aptitude tests measure the probability of a person's success in some unfamiliar area. A final exam in college is an example of an achievement test because the test measures information that has already been presented. Law enforcement promotion exams are usually in the form of an achievement test. In contrast, a college entrance test (such as the SAT Reasoning Test) is an example of an aptitude test because the test measures existing skills to predict one's ability to grasp and master information that will be presented at a later date. Entry-level law enforcement exams are more likely to be in the form of an aptitude test.

Usually studying previously presented material can improve performance on achievement tests. However, little can be done to quickly improve performance on aptitude tests. This is because aptitude tests measure existing skills that have been developed over a long period of time. If an individual is weak in the areas associated with successful performance, the aptitude test will detect these weaknesses and render scores that reflect a decreased probability of success. The only way to predictably improve scores on an aptitude test is to improve existing skills through extensive learning and practice (e.g., coursework, training).[94]

This information renders the proverbial good news/bad news dilemma. The good news is that you do not need to waste your time with cramming prior to an entrance level law enforcement exam. The bad news is that it takes a lot of work to improve a low score. Here is what I would do. Take reasonable steps to familiarize yourself with the test protocol and sample questions for an aptitude test. Most agencies supply a study guide for this purpose. If no study guide is available, someone is likely to be selling a book on the topic. A limited amount of preparation will help immensely but you will quickly run up against diminishing returns.

CBP has two good examples of entry-level exams. The first is the written test for the CBP Officer position. CBP provides a manual to help prepare applicants for the test. The manual will familiarize you with the Logical Reasoning Test, the Arithmetic Reasoning Test, and the Writing Skills Test and will give you a chance to study some sample questions and explanations for the correct answers to each question. If you have not had much practice taking written, multiple-choice tests, you will have an opportunity to see what the tests look like and to practice taking questions similar to those on the tests.[95]

---

[94]http://www.post.ca.gov/selection/poWrittenPracticeTest.pdf
[95]http://www.cbp.gov/linkhandler/cgov/careers/study_guides/guides_supervisory/entry_guide/cprepmanual.ctt/cprepmanual.pdf

The CBP Officer Examination manual can be found by following this link: http://www.cbp.gov/linkhandler/cgov/careers/study_guides/guides_supervisory/entry_gui de/cprepmanual.ctt/cprepmanual.pdf. The second example from CBP is the Border Patrol Agent exam. There is also a preparation manual, which can be found by following this link: http://www.cbp.gov/xp/cgov/careers/study_guides/guides_bp/entry_guide/.

Applicants for the Secret Service Uniform Division and Capitol Police Officer positions must take the Police Officer's Selection Test (POST). The POST is an entry level basic skills test that helps law enforcement agencies select the most qualified applicants by ensuring that candidates possess the basic cognitive skills necessary to successfully perform the job. The POST is a valid, job related test designed specifically for law enforcement use, which measures these basic skills: Arithmetic, Reading Comprehension, Grammar, and Incident Report Writing.

Special Agent applicants for the IRS, Secret Service, and BATF must take the Treasury Enforcement Agent (TEA) Exam. Even though BATF is now under the Department of Justice, they still use the TEA Exam. There are a number of books available as study guides for the TEA Exam. The Marshals Service no longer administers the Deputy Marshals Exam and now hire predominantly through various intern programs and Merit Promotions without the use of a written exam.

Physical Tests

The premise behind physical testing is the judicial system has recognized the requirement for law enforcement officers to maintain high levels of physical fitness to perform essential and critical job functions. The difficulty for an agency is to validate the relationship between the physical requirements and various essential job functions. The easiest tests to administer may not necessarily have the best correlation to the essential job functions. My advice for applicants on physical tests is to find out about the agency requirements for their specific test. Then consult appropriate medical professionals and after begin training for the specific agency physical test as many months in advance of the test as possible. If you are not sure how to train for the events, consult a fitness specialist. Given enough preparation, even persons in poor physical condition can improve and score very high on an agency physical test.

Two examples with contrasting but acceptable methods of physical testing are listed in the following text. The first physical test is for Border Patrol Agents and the second is for FBI Special Agents. The Border test does not differentiate between male and female test takers. There is one standard for both genders. The FBI test, on the other hand, does have a different standard for both genders. Some physical tests even have different standards based on the applicant's gender and age.

The Border Patrol has one of the best recruit physical testing programs of all the federal agencies. The Border Patrol currently has a pass/fail physical requirement of 20 push-ups in 60 seconds, 25 sit-ups in 60 seconds and a 30 step per minute step-test for five minutes.[96] After the applicant is hired but before graduating from the Border Patrol Academy, the new recruit must also pass a task related physical test in the form of the Border Patrol Confidence Course and 1.5 mile timed run. Some of the obstacles in the Border Patrol Confidence Course include a six-foot wall climb, a log walk (balance), jumping into and through a simulated open railroad car, low crawling, a hand-over-hand climb, and climbing up a ladder with the entire course completed within a specific time frame. In the Border Patrol, physical tests there are no separate standards for different age groups or genders.

In comparison, FBI Special Agent applicants must pass a physical test consisting of four mandatory events that are administered in the following order:

- Maximum number of sit-ups in one minute;
- Timed 300 meter sprint ;
- Maximum number of push-ups (not timed);
- Timed 1½ mile run ;

A FBI Special Agent applicant will have three opportunities to achieve a passing score on the Physical Fitness Test. There is a strictly defined scoring scale and protocol for each event with different scores for men and women. In order to pass the Physical Fitness Test, Special Agent applicants must achieve a minimum cumulative score of twelve points with at least one point in each of the four events. New Agent Trainees admitted to the FBI Academy must re-pass the Physical Fitness Test in their first week at the Academy. The test, scoring scale, and protocol are the same, except a fifth event is added, standard pull-ups. The score on pull-ups is not used for pass/fail purposes, but is used by the FBI Training Division for fitness awards, including the 50-point award.[97]

Some agencies do not use any physical tests in the job application process but almost all federal law enforcement agencies promote fitness to their officers through voluntary or mandatory fitness and wellness programs. It is worth repeating, the good news for applicants is that given enough time, persons in very poor physical condition can change to become highly fit individuals likely to score well on any agency physical test. Even when an agency does not use physical tests in the application process, right or wrong, your physical appearance will provide an impression during any face-to-face interview.

---

[96]

http://www.cbp.gov/linkhandler/cgov/careers/customs_careers/border_careers/fitness_requirements/bp_agent_fit.ctt/bp_agent_fit.pdf

[97] http://www.fbijobs.gov/1113.asp#1

If you are unsure of which agency you may apply for, but want to practice doing a fitness test, a good generic test can be found at:
 http://www.fletc.gov/training/programs/physical-techniques-division/requirement-documents/physical-efficiency-battery-peb.html.

Assessment interviews are another type of common assembled examinations for entry-level positions. Rather than addressing it here, it is covered as a part of the Interviews Chapter coming up next.

Unassembled Examinations

The two main types of unassembled examinations are KSAs and questionnaires. The recent trend for career advancement and job announcements with only a few positions to fill is to use web-based questionnaires. The third type of unassembled examination is a work sample; although, I have never yet seen work samples used as part of the law enforcement examination process to determine who makes the best-qualified list. I have seen work samples used as part of the selection process to determine who is selected off the best-qualified list (certificate).

KSAs

KSA are used almost exclusively for Merit Promotion Vacancy Announcement rather than All Sources Vacancy Announcements. Before the recent move toward Web based applications, job seekers completed paper (hard copies) of their federal resume and written narratives responding to KSA questions. Then, they would mail their resumes and KSAs to the human resource office listed in the vacancy announcement. The older style federal resumes include the SF 171 and the OF 612. Under a traditional application processes, an applicant examination consisted of a rating panel grading the applicant's KSA against a crediting plan. A crediting plan is a matrix that defines how many points an applicant receives types of experience written in the applicants KSA answers.

Like it or not, writing is a huge amount of the process for federal job applicants under the traditional KSA system. In fact, an entire industry of federal application writers now exists to help applicants with their writing dilemmas. These are professional writers who have "been there and done that" with resumes and will try to wordsmith your paperwork to improve your odds of making the best-qualified list. While I have never used these services myself, I can tell you that some applicants really do need help with their technical writing and the use of these services is not unethical. Many people believe that certain buzzwords give them credit in the KSA system. I have not found that to be true.

Throughout my career, I have served on dozens of rating and ranking panels to review KSA narratives. I have seen the good the bad and the ugly. Unfortunately, some applicants have poorly prepared paperwork with grammar and spelling mistakes as well as typographical errors. While I expect to see a few errors in a document 150 pages long, I do not expect it on a 2-page KSA narrative. Just as bad, many applicants would fail to properly write about the KSA questions. If you are a poor writer, take classes on technical writing or pay someone to professionally write your resume and KSAs.

Good KSA narratives describe your actual knowledge, skills, and abilities and use examples with a description of results achieved. Unfortunately, many federal employees attempt to write their KSAs by copy and pasting from their current position description, which describes responsibilities and duties rather than knowledge, skills, and abilities. It is important to review the job duties for the position, which you are applying, as it will provide you with clues and keywords to use in your KSA narratives. The worst mistake you can make on your KSA is to lie regarding your accomplishments. Writing a falsehood on your resume or KSA can lead to administrative disciplinary action, possibly employment termination. On the other hand, it is important to be boastful to the point that would be considered bragging and in poor taste for any other forum. It is OK to brag as long as you can back it up. This is the one time where modesty and being humble is not recommended.[98]

There is a good article available on the Internet that expands upon the previous paragraph. It is titled Applying *for a Promotion or New Job? Don't Make These Mistakes on Your Resume!* and can be found at http://www.fedsmith.com/article/1328/. You will likely have to register for the free newsletter before you can view the article. I have more advice on KSAs in the chapter titled, Techniques, Tactics, and Strategies. The FBI also provides a helpful web page on how to prepare resumes when applying for positions with that agency. http://www.fbijobs.gov/031.asp#3

QuickHire® (Questionnaire)

The QuickHire® system is a publicly available Web site through which applicants can provide information, apply for jobs, and track status; it also enables human resources personnel to process the receipt of applicants, rate and rank applicants, communicate internally with hiring authorities, notify applicants of status, and overall streamline the hiring process. Applicants may enter the QuickHire® system through consolidated online government job boards, such as through www.USAJobs.com. If an applicant requests to apply for a job, that applicant's Web browser is forwarded to the separate QuickHire® Web site. QuickHire® has the flexibility to use KSA type written narratives or run in a fully automated mode based on a questionnaire. Because KSAs have to be manually rated and ranked, most agencies prefer the questionnaire format in the QuickHire® system.

---

[98]http://www.fedsmith.com/article/1328/, August 8, 2007, Applying for a Promotion or New Job? Don't Make These Mistakes on Your Resume!By John Grobe

Questionnaires use yes/no, true/false, and multiple choice questions which are rated and ranked by a computer. Most of the questions are derived from job tasks and position descriptions. Questions may also ask about accomplishments, which demonstrate knowledge, skill, and abilities. In the full auto mode, each question has a score and a weighting and all of the responses for an applicant are added to provide their assessment score to include applicable veterans' preference points. More than a decade ago, the Customs Service used bubble sheet type questionnaires where the respondent would use a number 2 pencil and shade in the correct corresponding oval to the question being asked about their experience in specific areas. QuickHire® does the same thing except it is done online.

I have applied for only one job using the QuickHire® system and found it to be much easier than the KSA style. The most visible point that applicants will notice when using QuickHire® is there are a series of questions and choices for you to answer. There may also be narratives for the respondent to provide examples of experience in specific areas. These narratives are generally not in the form of KSA questions, rather they are an explanation or example of a statement the respondent has given a positive response to. For example, on a recent application using QuickHire®, I indicated that I possessed skill in preventing, detecting, and investigating felony crimes. Following that question, I was prompted to write 500 words or less, an example describing my skill in preventing, detecting, and investigating felony crimes. In this example, the narrative was not scored but rather used to verify the previous question. The narratives are also a likely source of questions during the next step, the interview.

In the full auto mode of QuickHire®, it does not take a Brain Surgeon to figure out which answers will provide the greatest amount of points to achieve the highest score. Here in lies the biggest drawback to the QuickHire® system or with any questionnaire process. Even before the QuickHire® days, there was a general problem of exaggeration by applicants when answering yes/no, true/false, and multiple-choice questions.

In one situation, I recall a few coworkers laughing in hysterics as we watched a fellow Inspector complete a questionnaire and listened to his rationalization of answers. I do not recommend completing these documents in a public forum but the point of the matter is there is a strong tendency to exaggerate answers. You may want to discuss any tenuous questions with a confidant before committing to the answer. The QuickHire® application that I completed had the following warning: "Any exaggeration of your experience, false statements, or attempts to conceal information may be grounds for not hiring you, or for firing you after you begin work."

The real difficulty is with the exact meaning of words. For example, in a QuickHire® assessment it asked if I routinely met with senior officials to discuss policy issues. What is the meaning of senior? Senior to me? The Senior Executive Staff. Does it mean the Senior Instructors that I supervise? How often is routinely? I did check the box indicating that I routinely did what it had asked. I also wrote notes next to each question for my own satisfaction so I will not be caught in situation during an interview where I am unable to explain my response to the question.

The best resume and the highest score on a merit promotion certificate does not necessarily get you the job. It usually only gets you to the next step which is a selection interview. Read on!

Chapter 9: Interviews

In any job interview, the employer is trying to obtain specific information about the potential employee. From my viewpoint, there are three categories of interviews you are likely to have for a federal law enforcement job. They are:

1. Assessment Interviews,
2. Selection Interviews, and
3. Background Investigation Interviews.

I highly doubt that you will find the categories I have listed in an interview book even though there are entire books devoted to the sole topic of job interviewing. Most interviewing articles and books will have categories like; informational interviews, structured and unstructured interviews, stress interviews, situational interviews, and targeted interviews. I do recommend reading and studying information on topics such as interviewing; however, there comes a point of diminishing returns. Keep in mind that your goal is not to be an expert on different types of interviews; it is to be a great interviewee for a federal law enforcement job.

In my experience, all government interviews are structured and are likely to have at least a few questions that put you under stress with scenarios or simply by the personal nature of the questions, e.g., tell me about your prior drug use. As a professional law enforcement trainer, my advice is to practice interviewing with a mirror until you are confident that you have a winning presentation. Repetition is the mother of skill. With most things in life there is a steep learning curve, the tenth time you do something will be much better than the first. Be sure to read specific advice provided for face-to-face interviews and phone interviews in the next chapter, Techniques, Tactics, and Strategies. Before you jump ahead, you will need a basic understanding of the purpose behind the three types of federal law enforcement interviews bulleted above.

The purpose and importance behind an interview will greatly vary depending on the type of interview and whether the job is entry level or a promotion. Entry-level assessment interviews are make or break for the applicant whereas selection interviews for a promotion are of much less importance. The reasoning behind this is that managers making a decision for a promotion should place a greater value on an employee's demonstrated work history rather than a one-hour interview. In fact, I would argue that an interview for a promotion with known candidates could only hurt the good employee who happens to be a poor interviewer. Simply said: "The best indicator for a manager of an employee's future success is to look at their past performance." Having said that, selection interviews with known applicants for a promotion are often done to give the appearance there is not a preselected candidate.

Contrary to what you may have been told, during the interview is not the time to ask about salary, housing relocation expenses, or anything else that you may think is negotiable. I do recommend asking insightful questions that will show you are familiar with the agency and their current events; this wants to be done in a manner that is not contrived but rather in a way that makes you look intelligent. Beyond that, there is really only one question that should be asked if you do not already know the answer and that is, when do you expect a selection to be made? Given the right circumstances, you may inquire about hanging around after the interview to talk with some of the agency's officers to find out more about the job.

Assessment Interviews

More often than not, assessment interviews are done for entry-level positions, they are almost never done for career advancement positions. Keep in mind an assessment interview is part of the numerical or pass/fail scoring that is used for ranking applicants and finding the best job candidates. Providing a numerical score for an interview is problematic so pass/fail is most often used. For entry-level law enforcement jobs, you should also expect some general integrity questions about arrests, convictions, and previous jobs. Other integrity questions will be in the form of scenarios such as:

- What would you do if you found out a coworker was showing up to work with alcohol on his or her breath?
- What would you do if while off duty and not in uniform you are inside your local bank and come across an armed bank robbery in progress?
- What would you do if a close relative asked you to look up and provide confidential information from a government computer database?

With most scenario based interview questions, the government is trying to determine if you fall within an acceptable range of responses. A coworker with alcohol on his breath should probably be handled without informing supervisors. Of course, this depends upon the amount of alcohol involved. After confronting your coworker with your suspicions, if you still suspect alcohol, suggest that your coworker take sick leave and that he or she go home. Forewarn him or her that in any future alcohol situation you will have to go to your supervisor.

In the second scenario, the Feds do not want a cowboy that is going to single handedly disarm bank robbers. Without a badge and a gun your role is simply to be, a good witness unless the bank robbers are active shooters (most armed bank robbers get in and out without shooting anyone). In the third scenario, it is common sense that you would not share confidential information from work with anyone that does not have the proper security clearance and the need to know the information. Do not overreact and call internal affairs on your brother unless it involves treason or another serious crime.

Few people should be failing their assessment interviews. If there is a point value for the assessment interview, these points are averaged or added to other points you have scored from other examinations, e.g., written test, physical abilities test, and KSAs. Pass/fail assessment interviews allow your other examinations to count. In either case, if your assessment score is high enough, your name will be sent forth on a certificate to the hiring officials. The selecting official may then choose to do a selection interview. In some cases, a great assessment interview may even pique the interest of an official to try to find a noncompetitive hiring authority that can be used to make a selection.

Selection Interviews

While unbeknown to most interviewees, the purpose of a selection interview is fundamentally different from an assessment interview. A selection interview is an interview of an applicant whose name is already on a certificate. Selection interviews are most often done for Merit Promotion Vacancy Announcements. There is no requirement for a selection interview; an applicant's name can be chosen the job from the certificate without doing an interview. The hiring officials can choose to interview only one name on the certificate, multiple names on the certificate, or none at all.

Any interview is a lengthy process and interviewers do not like to waste their time interviewing people they do not intend to hire. Therefore, these interviews are a great opportunity for the applicant because it means there is a reasonable chance they may be selected. While these interviews can be scored/graded, it is more common that interviewing officials do not keep any score for a selection interview. The reason for not grading or scoring an assessment interview is quite simple, it is not required and any scoring system opens up the possibility of someone challenging the process or outcome.

In most selection interviews, the interviewers unofficially keep track in their heads and write notes on paper to applicant Q&A responses. The interviewers know which person or persons they will recommend for selection even though there is not a score or grade. Selection interviews allow for latitude on the part of the hiring official. Expect questions like:

- Briefly describe your prior law enforcement work experiences.
- What makes you the best qualified for this job?
- What special qualifications or certifications do you have?
- Why do you want to leave your current job?

The federal government is very big on trying to hire based on knowledge, skills, and abilities for Merit Promotion Vacancy Announcements. Therefore, definitely expect questions related to the KSAs if they were used in the vacancy announcement. If you applied for a vacancy announcement using a QuickHire® questionnaire, many selection interview questions will come directly from those questions. There will likely also be questions about job attributes and special qualifications that you bring to the table. Included at the end of this Chapter are many possible interview questions.

Personality plays a big factor in an assessment interview even though it may not officially be a part of the interview. This is particularly true in situations where the agency wants you to spend an extended period of time with them. At a seminar I attended regarding government hiring practices, the presenter made it a key learning point that private industry does much better than government with regard to hiring based on personalities or how well the applicant will "fit in." It was his belief the government lacked a key element when it hires people, chiefly: Will the employee's personality work well in the organization? I did not want to stand up and voice my disagreement so I kept quiet and discussed this with my colleagues later in the day.

My coworkers and I believe the personality and fitting-in issues become self-evident in any selection interview. While you may not see personality type questions on a federal job interview, you can be guaranteed that one of the first thoughts running through an interviewer's head after its completion is. Would I want to work with this person? That should come as no surprise since the hiring agency's own officers conduct most interviews and they may in fact be working with the applicants they recommend.

Some words of wisdom for an interview, every pessimist I know believes they are a realist. Reserved optimism is the rule of the day for interviews. Do not bad mouth your current employer or present any negative comments about coworkers. There are ways to say things with a positive spin. For example: "I want to work for an agency that has a great mission" or "I'm looking forward to new career challenges and working with an agency that is well respected" is better than saying "my current job sucks" or "my boss has been riding me so I'm looking for a change".

The questions on the following pages are examples you may encounter during a selection interview. How would you answer them?

- Why did you become interested in law enforcement?
- What do you know about our organization?
- What do you know about this position?
- Have you discussed the duties/requirements of this position with anyone performing similar work? If so, who?
- Have you read the position description for this job?
- If you are selected, what do you think would be expected of you?
- What do you think would be the most difficult part of adjusting to this position?
- Why did you apply for this position?
- Discuss duties of your present job and/or any other jobs you have held which would help you perform successfully in the position you are seeking?
- Have you had any training or experience in the field of law enforcement? What type of training?
- What outside activities are you involved in?
- Have you held any leadership positions? If so, describe.
- Have you ever organized individuals to accomplish a goal? If so, explain.
- What hobbies or outside interests do you have which would help you in the performance of this job?
- What have you done that shows initiative, persistence, and willingness to work hard in order to accomplish a goal?
- In your work experience, schooling, or outside activities, what accomplishments are you especially proud of?
- What are your career goals?
- What position would you like to hold in the future?
- In what way does this job meet (or lead you towards) your career goals?
- What do you regard to be some of your shortcomings and developmental needs?
- What factors in your past work experience, education or other activities do you feel will contribute to your ability to learn and advance in law enforcement?
- Describe your last training experience (formal, OJT, correspondence course, etc.).
- Did you complete the training? If not, why?
- In considering joining our organization, what are some of the factors that you take into account?
- Why do you think you might like to work for this agency?
- Why did you choose your particular field of study?
- What courses did you like best? Least? Why?
- Have you ever changed your major field of interest? If so, why?
- What courses did you start and later drop? Why?
- Discuss some of your term papers, theses or special projects.
- In what school activities have, you participated? Why?
- Which did you enjoy most?
- How did they change over the course of your education?
- What positions of leadership have you attained?
- How successful were you in achieving the goals of the groups you headed?
- What are your plans for further education?

- What have you done that shows initiative, persistence, and willingness to work hard in order to accomplish a goal?
- Do you prefer working with others or by yourself?
- In what type of position are you most interested?
- In what way has your education and training prepared you for a law enforcement position?
- What qualifications do you have that make you feel that you will be successful in law enforcement?
- Tell me about your present job. What do you like best about it? What do you like least? What frustrates you about it? What have you learned on this job?
- Where do you rank your present job with other jobs you have held? Why?
- What are some of the things in a job that are important to you?
- In general, what type of work have you enjoyed the most? The least? Why?
- Within a work environment, what are your strengths? Your weaknesses?
- For what things have, your supervisors complimented you?
- What are some problems you encountered on the job? How did you solve these problems?
- What are some of your more important accomplishments?
- What are the reasons you were successful in achieving these accomplishments?
- Were there any unusual difficulties you had to overcome to achieve these accomplishments?
- What are some important decisions or recommendations you are called upon to make?
- What decisions are easiest for you to make? Which are more difficult?
- How has your previous work experience helped you to improve your decision-making abilities?
- Cite an important decision, which you would make differently if you could do it over again.
- Do you prefer working with others or working independently? Why?
- Considering your relationship with co-workers, customers, supervisors, etc.;
  - Cite an example of how you have been effective in relating with others.
  - Cite an example of how you might not have been particularly effective.
  - What might you do differently next time in that situation?
- How do you prioritize your work?
- How well do you work under pressure?
- Cite an example of a pressure situation you faced on the job.
- How did you handle it?
- What motivates you?
- What computers/software packages have you worked with?
- For what purpose?
- What computer training have you had?
- What was your most difficult assignment?
- What was your most rewarding assignment?
- What are your short-term goals?
- What are your long-term goals?
- Have your long-term goals changed in recent years? If so, how?

- What are you doing to achieve your long-term objectives?
- Which kind of supervisor gets the best performance out of you?
- Describe your relationship with your supervisor.
- Regarding the vacant law enforcement position: Why are you interested in the position?
- What is your background particularly qualifies you for this job?
- Why do you think you would be good in this position?
- Are there any reasons why you might not be able to perform the duties of this position? If so, explain.
- How do you feel about ...using a firearm to defend yourself or others? ...Working overtime? Working on a particular work schedule? Travel?
- Do you have any other special qualifications relating to this position that I should know about?
- What questions do you have for me?

Selection Interview Questions - Career Advancement

- What are you seeking in this position that you are not getting in your present job?
- Why do you want to make a career/job change at this time?
- Discuss some special assignments or projects you have worked on.
- How were you selected for the assignment?
- Did you work on the assignment alone or with others?
- Discuss some of your most significant career accomplishments. Concentrate on those within the last five years.
- Most of us can look back on a new idea or innovation we feel proud introducing. Describe one or two such innovations you are particularly proud of.
- What changes have you made in the nature of your job during the period that you have held it?
- What was the toughest assignment you have had? What factors made it so difficult? How did you handle it?
- How much leeway does your supervisor give you in working out problems?
- Cite some examples of important decisions or recommendations you are called upon to make.
- How do you go about making these decisions/recommendations? (With whom do you talk?)
- As you have gained greater experience, how have you improved in your decision-making abilities?
- Considering your work relationships both inside and outside the agency, how have you been particularly effective in relating with others?
- In what ways have, you contributed to your organization's success?
- What computer/software packages/automated systems have you worked with?
- What planning or data management functions did you use them for?
- How have computers helped you to better accomplish your work?
- What have you done about your career development in the last few years?
- What were your long-term career goals?
- How have they changed over the years?

- What are you doing to help accomplish your current career goals?
- In what way has your present job prepared you for greater responsibilities?
- What in your background particularly qualifies you for this job?

Selection Interview Questions - Career Advancement (Supervisory)

- How do you view the job of a supervisor?
- Why do you feel you have management potential?
- How many people have you supervised/led: In your current job? In previous jobs?
- What types of positions have you supervised/led?
- Describe your supervisory responsibilities and the extent of your authority.
- Describe your leadership style.
- What do you like best about being a supervisor? What do you like least?
- What responsibility did you have in recruiting and selecting your staff?
- What criteria did you use in making hiring decisions?
- What type of problems have you faced in directing work groups?
    How did you handle them?
    What was the outcome?
- How would you handle a situation where one of your workers changes from a reliable, hardworking employee to a problem person?
- Describe your method of motivating people.
- Which approaches have worked best?
- Which approaches have failed?
- How do you get the best work from your subordinates?
- What responsibility have you had in orienting and training new people?
- Some managers keep a very close check on their organization. Others use a loose rein. What pattern do you follow?
- How do you convey information to your people?
- How do you maintain discipline in your organization?
- What types of discipline problems have you had to deal with?
- How did you handle them?
- How is your group's morale?
- On what do you base your opinion?
- What planning processes have you found useful?
- In what way do you feel you have improved in your planning abilities/methods?
- What systems and procedures have you developed to improve the efficiency of your organization? How well did they work?
- What experience have you had dealing with unions/labor relations?
- Are you familiar with the negotiated agreement?
- What do you know about the EEO program?
- What are your personal EEO contributions?
- How does your experience bear on your qualification for this position?
- What things do you think would contribute to your effectiveness as a supervisor?
- What things might interfere with your effectiveness as a supervisor?
- What are the two or three most important things you have learned as a supervisor?

- What would you recommend that would help this organization to more effectively accomplish its mission?

Background Investigation Interview

Almost all federal law enforcement jobs require a background investigation for security and suitability purposes. Your background interview answers should sound sincere and not look like you are trying to hide anything. A deer in the headlights look is not the image you want to portray. How would you respond to the question: "When was the last time you used marijuana?" Be polite, courteous, and truthful. For most law enforcement background checks, the interviewer will be corroborating much of what is stated through interviews with coworkers, relatives, neighbors, roommates, and spouses.

Now is not the time to joke or have any behavioral outbursts. You have the job as long as what you say matches up with what the investigator finds out and you are within the boundaries of the agencies security and suitability limitations. The investigator does not have the option of overlooking something that is unfavorable. It is his or her job to issue a report stating the facts, not to make a decision about your suitability. You may be able to talk a traffic cop out of a speeding ticket, but that is not the case with the background investigator.

The SF86 will be the main source of the background investigator's questions. You will be asked to explain any missing information, reasons for leaving previous jobs, periods of time where you have not listed a place of residence, foreign travel, and many other questions. It is not uncommon for the investigator to call you back to get clarification on various issues. Do not be overly concerned if the investigator calls on you a few times, it is their job to complete the puzzle and find all the missing pieces to provide a full and accurate report.

Chapter 10: Techniques, Tactics, and Strategies

Just as in law enforcement situations where there are techniques, tactics, and strategies that can improve your odds of surviving and winning, there are specific techniques, tactics, and strategies that you can use when trying to get a federal law enforcement job that will improve your odds of success. I am not suggesting any underhanded tricks or unethical methods but rather rock solid sound advice gained throughout a 20-year career on both sides of the hiring table. Can you be hired without following these suggestions? Sure! However, make it easy on yourself and stack the odds in your favor.

With over 10 million visitors each month to the USAJobs Web site you must try techniques, tactics, and strategies that will make your application stand out above the others.

Get a College Degree

A Bachelor's of Science or Arts degree from an accredited college may be one of the single best things you can do to increase your odds of getting a federal law enforcement job. Any college or university will suffice as long as it is accredited. Do not attempt the route of a diploma mill where you pay money and provide the school with your "life experiences" which results in a bogus college certificate. The federal government is on the lookout for this and a background investigation will weed you out quickly. However, my experience has been that a degree from an accredited online institution is as good as any other if it is accredited. Distributed educational opportunities such as online colleges nearly eliminate all excuses for not getting a degree. While many younger students are caught up in the prestige of fancy label schools, a degree really is a common commodity. The pedigree just does not matter, unless it is an Ivy League university or United States Military Academy.

A Criminal Justice degree is usually better than most others are if you intend to go into federal law enforcement. Yes, the FBI likes to hire people with law degrees, accounting, and other specialized fields. Forensic Science or specialized language studies are also other areas of study to consider. If you have, a desire to work for natural resource type agencies you may want to consider Zoology as a degree.

Advanced degrees such as a Masters or Doctorate are definitely a bonus; however, graduate degrees are unnecessary for entry-level law enforcement positions. Practical experience may provide you a better return on investment. It is important to start applying for internships as soon as possible; usually this is in the Junior or Senior year of college. GPA is also a very important aspect for entry into federal internships. Some internships require a minimum GPA of 3.5 on a 4.0 scale. Participation in extracurricular activities such as honor societies and criminal justice organizations will also help improve your job prospects.

My experience regarding promotions and lateral transfers in uniformed positions is that a college degree is usually a minor consideration while the most important criteria is your current work ethic and quality. At middle management and Senior Executive levels, a college degree becomes increasingly more important.

Gain Career or Career Conditional Status

There are many non-law enforcement jobs with the federal government that will provide you with the all-important Career/Career Conditional status. This status allows you to apply for Merit Promotion Vacancy Announcements. Remember, Merit Promotion Vacancy Announcements are very much a level playing field, as veterans are not provided veterans' preference examination points. Career or Career Conditional status is like a property right. You get the status by being a federal employee in a Competitive Service appointment. Preferably, the non-law enforcement federal job you acquire will be in the same agency as the law enforcement job that you really want. The advantage of using this strategy is that you start your federal time clock, earn a paycheck, and learn more about the agency. The only disadvantage is that some agencies tend to tight cast employees into categories so that a clerical worker may have a hard time being viewed as a law enforcement officer by the hiring officials. This is similar to the FBI not providing their uniformed officers a career path to become Special Agents.

As an example of this strategy, your end goal may be to become a Marine Interdiction Agent (MIA) with Customs and Border Protection. If you are having no success applying directly for the MIA jobs, you may want to try an indirect approach. Apply for the lower graded Mission Support Assistant positions with CBP. As a Mission Support Assistant, you will provide assistance in one or more of the administrative support areas (e.g., finance and budget, logistics and procurement, human resources, records and files management, etc.). Duties include maintaining tracking systems of transactions, coordinating requests for services from users and completing necessary forms, procuring routine equipment and services, maintaining office files and records, and preparing recurring reports. Good things will happen if you excel at the lower graded positions and a reputation of being punctual, hardworking, energetic, detail oriented, and easy to get along with will open up career advancement opportunities such as the MIA jobs.

Improve Your Writing Skills

There is a glaring deficiency in reading and writing among new entrants in the American workforce, and that is troubling employers who are being forced to invest in additional training...for one of the most fundamental job skills in the 21st century economy.[99] I would further add to this by stating that if you are looking for career advancement in law enforcement, good writing skills are essential and may be a key factor in differentiating job applicants. Most federal law enforcement officers have the commitment and dedication to improve their "sexy" job tasks like shooting, defensive tactics, and other enforcement related functions. After all, those are the things that make being in law enforcement exciting. Unfortunately, fewer officers take the necessary steps to improve

---

[99] http://www.workforce.com/section/00/article/25/27/49.html, *Jeremy Smerd*

their writing skills. More precisely, technical writing skills are needed to write memorandums, statements from witnesses, investigative reports, and of course the written narratives so often used in Merit Promotion Vacancy Announcements. At the very least, you can read books on the subject and ask others to review your work. Even better, take college technical writing classes.

Obtain Law Enforcement Experience

Law enforcement experience with state or local agencies is a great way to improve your resume. Unfortunately, it does not provide direct access to federal jobs. State and local experience does provide an individual with contacts and networking as well as insight into the various federal agencies. Most of the people I talk to about federal law enforcement jobs are state and local officers that are looking for more lucrative law enforcement positions with the federal government. The most often used path to federal employment that I have seen with state and local officers is to dovetail their non-federal police experience with a short military career.

Some Special Agent positions require investigative experience that is unlikely to be obtained in uniformed positions be it federal, State, or local agencies. In contrast, being a detective with a county or city agency may be the quickest method to satisfy the "investigative" experience requirement of some Special Agent positions.

Acquire Specialized Experience

Some federal law enforcement jobs require specialized experience. These requirements are listed in the vacancy announcements. Other positions, while not requiring specialized experience, through the examination process will give value to those who possess certain (specialized) knowledge, skills, and abilities. A few jobs that come to mind are CBP Air Interdiction Officers or Marine Interdiction Agents, ATF Bomb Technicians or Forensics Specialists, and K-9 Handlers with various agencies.

One of the most common methods to get this specialized experience is through service in the military. This requires a commitment that many are unwilling or unable to make. However, there are other ways to get the specialized experience. There are many flight schools where students can get their pilots license. With a years' worth of boating experience and knowledge of navigation rules, piloting, dead reckoning and other nautical skills, you can get your Coast Guard issued Captain's License.[100] Specialized experience may be what differentiates one applicant from another.

---

[100]http://www.fedsmith.com/article/1462/, New Year's Resolutions to Enhance Your Federal Career, By John Grobe Thursday, December 27, 2007

Join the Military

Enlisting in the military is certainly an option for those looking to use it as a stepping-stone to get into a civilian law enforcement career. All the branches of the military have career paths that will provide direct experience for federal civilian law enforcement positions. Certainly, people that can get into military investigative positions such as Army CID, Air Force OSI, Navy CIS, or Coast Guard CID will improve their odds for civilian Special Agent positions. Many Military Police and Shore Patrol types find their way to uniformed civilian law enforcement jobs. One of the greatest benefits provided to some military personnel is that of veterans' preferences. Having said all this, I would encourage exploring other options for getting a federal law enforcement job prior to enlisting. Going the military route is a long-term approach and not for the impulsive. The great thing about being in the military is that your time serving your country will usually count toward your federal civilian retirement. It may not necessarily count toward 6C-covered time but it can be added on top of the 6C-covered time once minimum retirement age and covered position time requirements are met.

Accept a Lower Pay Grade/Position

One of the best tactics for job applicants is to apply for any pay grade for the job you want. Typically entry-level positions advertise positions at multiple grade levels such as GS 5/7/9. In the application process, you must identify which grade(s) you are willing to accept. Obviously, you would prefer the highest paying job. The way the hiring process works, certificates (lists of names) for each grade (5, 7, and 9) are provided to the selecting official. There is no way a selecting official can choose a name that is not on the specific certificate he or she desires to hire from. By accepting a lower grade, your name may in fact show up on a best-qualified certificate so that a hiring official can select your name. The down side of course is that you may be accepting lower pay. This is temporary under most federal pay systems.

Another similar tactic is to apply for positions with a lower full performance grade. As discussed in Chapter 2, there is a generally accepted hierarchy in federal jobs. BOP Correctional Officers, CBP Officers, and Border Patrol Agent positions have a full performance grade lower than Special Agent positions with the Secret Service, ATF, Marshals, or ICE will bring more qualified job seekers and stiffer competition. While you may perceive that your talents are worthy of one of the more prestigious positions and agencies, your resume may not differentiate you from others applying for highly sought after jobs. However, that same resume with a less prestigious agency/job position may make you a top candidate. The cliché, big fish in a small pond comes to mind. In time, this may further allow you to stand out, thus increasing your chances to get the job that you really want.

Apply For Multiple Entry Level Positions

I am a big advocate of risk management when it comes to applying for entry-level jobs. Do not put all of your eggs in one basket. While I do not support a shotgun approach of applying for every job, applying for only one particular position is very risky. The idealism of wanting to work for one particular agency will wear off quickly when the reality of putting food on the table sets in. You can always apply for your dream job at some later point in time.

Many people erroneously believe that federal agencies talk to each other and know which other jobs an applicant is seeking. After all, an employer such as the Federal Government would frown upon applying for multiple jobs as it may indicate indecisiveness or lack of stability common sense. The truth of the matter is that agencies and even units within agencies are likely not to know you have applied for other entry-level positions and even if they did, they would likely not care. A friend and former classmate of mine had made it through ¾ of the basic Border Patrol Agent Academy when he received a job offer as a Customs Inspector. He took the Inspector job because it was physically located near his hometown of Buffalo, New York. About a year later, he was successful in getting his dream job as a New York State Trooper.

Many applicants have asked me whether management looks down switching between agencies upon. In my experiences, it only becomes a concern when it is frequent and done for no apparent reason. No one will fault you for trying to improve your lot in life. For example, a person has several applications outstanding for various jobs including the Border Patrol and the Secret Service. The Border Patrol job comes through with the first offer but the person's ultimate goal is a job as a Secret Service Special Agent. Take the first offer that comes along, the Secret Service can hire you even if you are currently in the other agency's basic training academy. One word of caution, don't mislead or lie to the recruiters and tell them that you have only applied for a position with their agency when in fact you have applications with other agencies.

Limit Applications for Promotion or Transfer

The opposite advice of applying for a few entry-level jobs is suggested for promotions or transfers; apply for only one job at any given time. You should expect that hiring officials from various jobs are likely to find out you have applied for other positions if the agency is centralized or if all of the job announcements go through a single human resource department. While applying for many different promotional opportunities in a given period should not be a bad thing, others may perceive it as a lack of commitment.

Their thought process may be, "Does he or she really want this job or does he or she really want the other job?" Even worse, once the word is out that you are seeking a transfer outside your current agency, it may be difficult if not impossible to get a promotion within. This even holds true in organizational units within the same agency. As an example: At FLETC there is a voluntarily applicant file in which current employees can place a resume so they may be considered for a reassignment at the same grade and pay to another Division (disciplines) within FLETC. Knowing that most instructor promotions at FLETC come from within a Division, I would expect a hiring official to question the commitment of an applicant for promotion who is trying to transfer out of the Division.

Take Assembled Written Examinations

There are a few reasons taking an assembled exam is a good tactic for getting a government job. Number one, assembled exams are often the main method an agency is using to hire for a particular position, especially entry level positions. Secondly, unlike unassembled exams where anyone can send in a resume to be examined, an assembled exam requires a time commitment and travel investment. Many qualified people will not be able to attend an assembled examination due to legitimate reasons. Others are simply apathetic or are unwilling to take time off from their current job for the opportunity to take a test. The third reason to take an assembled examination is that agencies sporadically offer these tests, which means that persons with less than perfect scores may be selected, albeit over a lengthy time lapse. There may be a fourth reason to take the written test and that is if you are one of those people who happen to perform well on cognitive exams. Agencies will often provide a study guide for the test.

- Treasury Enforcement Agent (TEA) Exam – by all accounts this is one of the hardest exams to take in terms of question difficulty. The IRS, Secret Service, and ATF Special Agent positions are some of the few remaining agencies using this exam. Some who have taken the exam recommend the study guide Master the Treasury Enforcement Agent (TEA) Exam by ARCO.
- Border Patrol Exam – For every 30 people who apply to take the Border Patrol's written exam, only one enters the Border Patrol Academy. Only about 40 percent of the applicants pass the exam. "It's a very difficult test," said Todd Bryant, acting assistant chief of Border Patrol's training and recruitment branch. Those who sign up for the test receive study guides, which they are strongly encouraged to use. "If you come in cold, though, your chances aren't good," Bryant said. The three-part exam tests applicants' logical reasoning skills and ability to learn a foreign language. Candidates are administered an "artificial language test," but a Spanish language proficiency test is substituted for those who believe they are already proficient in Spanish. The exam also includes an assessment of what you have learned from past work experiences. The test takes about 4½ hours....[101]

---

[101] http://www.armytimes.com/careers/second_careers/military_borderpatrol_070530/

Take Unassembled Examinations

Unassembled examinations that assess an applicant's written narratives on knowledge, skill, and ability questions are falling out of favor. The current trend for unassembled examinations is an automated process through a web-based system of questions and responses, e.g. QuickHire®. The traditional method has been for the applicant to write (typed) paragraphs about certain topics such as Knowledge of federal law enforcement procedures. Both these methods are somewhat flawed but represent great opportunities especially for an applicant who performs poorly on written multiple-choice tests. Regarding the traditional method of written KSAs, keep in mind these will be hand graded by a panel. For this reason alone, I recommend having each KSA topic at least one page but not more than two typed pages. Of course, the word "typed" means computer generated as opposed to an actual typewriter. No one hand writes these so do not even think about that as an option. The reason for keeping each KSA to not more than two pages is that a panel of raters will have to read everyone's KSAs and provide a score for each one. You do the math: five KSAs times 50 applicants equals 250 KSAs that must be read by each rating member. Trust me when I say that a rating official does not want to read a 10-page document on your Knowledge of federal law enforcement procedures. The opposite extreme is to write only one paragraph. This will likely get you the proverbial goose egg for a rating. One full page, two at the most.

- Knowledge: A body of information, usually of a factual or procedural nature, which, when applied, makes acceptable performance on the job possible.
- Skills: The proficient manual, verbal or mental manipulation people or objects. A skill can be observed quantified and improved with practice or training.
- Abilities: The power to perform an observable activity or behavior that results in an observable product or consequence.

Read the general description of the duties and responsibilities, read the list of KSAs. Look for clues to help you draw from your experiences the best example that matches what is required for the position. For example, if one of the KSAs listed is "Ability to communicate in writing," look at the duties and responsibilities and determine what the job requires you to write. If you can show specific past experience in writing the kinds of things required for the job, you would have a better chance of receiving a higher score on this particular KSA.

Write specific and detailed descriptions of your work experiences. Include answers to the following:

- An estimate of when the experience(s) was acquired.
- A description of the problem(s) you faced or the objectives(s) you were trying to accomplish.
- A specific statement of what you actually did.
- A description of the outcome or results of the activity.
- The name and telephone number of someone who can verify the information you provided. (This does not have to be a supervisor.)[102]

Address each KSA listed separately. Do not combine KSAs and give one answer. The response to each KSA should include a detailed narrative highlighting your experience, education and/or training, which further justifies that you possess the specific requirements for the position.

Write about your level of knowledge on the topic and practical situations where you have used that knowledge. Write about formal and informal education on the topic even indicating grades and awards received. Proper grammar and spelling is critical. The use of bulleted items and good organization of thoughts is very important.

Look to the Future

Commonly, vacancy announcements are open for a short period, and with any luck, you will find out about the vacancy early rather than near or after the closing date. You should have a prepared resume prior to finding out there is an open vacancy announcement to save you time so that you may focus your attention on more important issues such as preparing for the written examination or finalizing the KSAs. Do research to find out the examination process for the previous vacancy for the same job. If KSAs were used, prepare your KSAs based on the previous announcements' KSA in anticipation the next ones will be the same. It is unlikely the KSAs will change dramatically from one vacancy to another for the same position.

The same holds true for QuickHire® applications; you can go through the process as if you were applying and review the questionnaire but not actually apply. This will give you a heads-up for the types of experience you will need to gain so you will score high on some future examination. It is sort of like having the test in advance. For example, if your long-term goal is to work as a Law Enforcement Instructor at FLETC, then study a vacancy announcement for the position today. Then work on getting the necessary experience that will put you in a good position to get the job in the future.

---

[102]http://www.sec.gov/jobs/jobs_sampleres.shtml

Apply for Lower Tiered 6C Positions

Sometimes persons graduating from college have an unrealistic expectation regarding their marketability. As stated earlier, expect the more prestigious law enforcement positions will be more competitive. Knowing this and given the fact that you should try to get hired on with a 6C covered law enforcement position as soon as possible, it is good advice to aim for a 6C job that you may consider lower tiered. Covered positions give the employee the opportunity to transfer to other covered positions within and outside the agency, all the while accruing time for the benefit of a special retirement. Retirement after twenty years on the job and fifty years of age or twenty-five years on the job at any age. Wow! Talk about great benefits. For this reason, I highly encourage new job applicants that are within the age limitations to apply for the Border Patrol Agent position. While it may not have the glamor or overall attractiveness of a Special Agent position, it does accrue the same retirement benefits. Transferring within the federal government is relatively easy, and you may even gain career or career conditional status that allows you to apply for the Merit Promotion Vacancy Announcements to get your dream job.

Qualify For As Many Hiring Authorities as Possible

Simply put, the more hiring authorities you qualify for, the greater the odds a selecting official can choose your name. Most importantly is to qualify for a hiring authority that provides a noncompetitive selection. Regarding the process for Merit Promotion and All Sources Vacancy Announcements, it is worth discussing the behind the doors decisions that are made. Let us suppose that a selecting official has decided he is interested in hiring a particular person even before a vacancy announcement is advertised on USAJobs. We will call this person Lucky Larry. Let us also suppose that Larry is very fortunate in that he qualifies for a non-competitive hiring authority.

Although the agency may be required to advertise the position with a vacancy announcement, it does not have to hire anyone that applies for the vacancy announcement except possible CTAP, ICTAP employees (there usually are not any). After the agency considers all the persons on the certificates, the hiring officials are then free to select Lucky Larry. This is why it is common to see Merit Promotion Vacancy Announcements open for a short duration and only for, CTAP, ICTAP, VRA, 30% Disabled Vets, and ADA.

Some may view the selection of Lucky Larry as unethical. However, technically this is not a "preselection" of Larry because others were considered. In fact, it is a good human resource practice and an encouraged tactic for agency personnel to develop pools of applicants and to keep in contact with these potential employees.

It should not come as a surprise that some applicants will have contacts and influence in the hiring process. I am not referring to any illegal or inappropriate influence; rather, legitimate activity that can be used to promote one's self. The bottom line is that in order for influence to be effective it must reach the selecting and recommending officials. I view these contacts at three different levels: low, medium, and high.

The lowest levels of influence are those that come from subordinate employees. Agency personnel are often encouraged to recruit and find good candidates to fill vacancies. In fact, some agencies even offer cash awards to employees that help to recruit applicants that are eventually hired. It is a good idea for an agency to have a well-filled pool of candidates available to fill a vacancy should one come available. The greater the respect by the selecting official toward the employee referring an applicant, the greater the chance for the applicant's likelihood of success. Conversely, if employee A is not well respected, his suggesting that he has found a good potential applicant will likely fall upon deaf ears.

Peers, immediate supervisor, and friends of the selecting and recommending officials fall into the medium level of influence. Most influences at this level are well received and respected by the hiring officials. Selecting officials are likely to take a good hard look at applications recommended by their peers. This level of influence will often generate a selection interview. The process of going through the interview allows the hiring officials to save face: They can look their peer in the eye and tell him or her the applicant was given a fair shake at the job.

At the highest levels of influence are the recommendations from Senior Executives Staff, political types such as Congressman, and other government VIPs. While state and local VIP normally have less influence in the federal arena, their power can certainly cross over to the federal domain. Influences at the highest level will usually generate a selection interview and often a selection. I cannot imagine a situation where an agency could not find a position for someone with a personal recommendation from a Congressman.

If I were just now starting my career, knowing what I know now about federal employment, I might take the route of doing a lot of volunteer work for a member of Congress (MOC). This volunteer work is particularly important during election years. While technically it would be unethical for a quid pro quo (this for that) favor, it is certainly within reason for a MOC to recommend a hardworking, enthusiastic, and intelligent person for a federal law enforcement job.

Phone Interview Tactics

No one likes phone interviews, not the interviewer or the interviewees. If you are given the choice of a phone interview or face-to-face, always select to do it in person rather than over the phone. Unfortunately, there are times when phone interviews are the only option. There may be time and travel constraints that cannot be overcome. There are times when I have used mandatory phone interviews to whittle down a list of prospective candidates to a more manageable list. The shorter list was then used to provide names for the face-to-face interviews. For a federal law enforcement internship program, I used phone interviews as the only interview method. Three intern coordinators would ask questions to help determine who was selected for these prestigious positions.

We used phone interviews for internship positions because it was unlikely that persons from all over the country would travel a great distance at their expense just for the chance at an internship. Secondly, we had a large number of qualified applicants and in the end, it was easy to rationalize only doing phone interviews because we would have the intern for only 12 weeks rather than years of service that would be expected with a full-time equivalent employee. Keep in mind the following facts and advice for phone interviews:

- There is usually more than one interviewer so be sure to write their names to help you remember them during the interview. Use their names sporadically and err on the side of formality rather than using their first names (unless asked to),
- You should not use a cell phone or any other phone that may drop the call or have a bad connection. Remember, the interview process may take a half-hour or longer. Use a landline in a quiet place where you will not be interrupted,
- Use notes unless told specifically not to and try to avoid the shuffling of paper. Your notes should contain questions and answers that you will likely be asked. Also, write down insightful questions that show your interest and knowledge about the position. Base your questions from recent reputable news articles or the agency's Web site. The best source might be the agency's strategic plan, which may be found through an Internet search engine.
- Long pauses and gaps in conversation are somewhat expected in a phone interview and are usually not as bad as they seem to the interviewee, the smoother you can make the conversation without rambling, the better.
- Avoid slang, word whiskers (words that you use repeatedly repeatedly), and filler sounds like "aaah" or "ummm."

It is worth repeating that we are rarely ever successful at anything attempted for the very first time unless we have practiced. Do not learn from your mistakes the hard way such as during a real telephone interview for a job you really want. Phone interviews can be practiced realistically with a friend and it is a painless way to make mistakes and learn this unique interviewing skill. Develop a list of questions you think will be asked and have a friend call you as role playing practice. Practice the interviews several times, at least until you eliminate any fatal errors.

Face-to-Face Interview Tactics-Image is everything

In the beginning of Andre Agassi's tennis career, his mantra was "image is everything" and this cliché is particularly true for law enforcement job seekers. The federal government is one of the best regarding the use of objective competency based hiring processes but the reality is, how you look will play a big factor in whether or not you get a job offer. This may in fact be a similar phenomenon to that revealed by studies showing attractive people literally and figuratively get doors opened and favors done for them by strangers. Interviewers and other recruiting and hiring decision makers see and talk to hordes of would be employees. Given the limited amount of time spent with any one applicant it is only natural they will try to come to quick decisions in their own mind regarding your future employment prospects regardless of the objective tests. Therefore, the first visual impression is critical.

Take a close look at the employees for the agency you want to join. What style of clothing do they wear and how is their hairstyle? Almost without exception, the employees of federal law enforcement agencies look very conservative, particularly new recruits. The exceptions are undercover cops and some officers working for natural resource agencies. Have ever noticed the Secret Service agents protecting the President? That is the image you want to mimic. Some federal agencies do have grooming standards but your best indicator is to use current employees as a benchmark.

From my experience at the largest law enforcement academy in the world, there are not many mullets, Afros, poufy, or high maintenance quaffs in the new recruits coming through basic training. I know, you know, and the interviewers know that how someone looks has nothing to do with their ability to do the job. The fact remains that you have a choice; conform to an image the agencies embrace or take your chances that your exceptional talents will be enough to get you hired or promoted. Other image issues include facial hair, tattoos, body piercings, jewelry, and physical shape.

A word or two on tattoos, as many as 16 percent of adult Americans have them. The Marines and the other branches of the military already ban tattoos that could be offensive or disruptive, such as images that are sexist, vulgar, gang related or extremist. The Navy decreed that tattoos visible while in short sleeve uniform cannot be larger than the wearer's hand. The Air Force says tattoos should be covered if they are bigger than ¼ the size of the exposed body part. Meanwhile, the Army has gone in the other direction, having relaxed its tattoo restrictions.[103]

---

[103] http://www.fedsmith.com/article/1279/, Dress Codes, Tattoos, and Federal Employees: A Brave New World by Steve Oppermann, Thursday, June 14, 2007

During an interview for a law enforcement job, most tattoos will be covered by attire such as a business suit and therefore they may go unnoticed by the interviewer. However, they will be readily apparent during fitness testing which officers in the agency often administer. As far as tattoos are concerned, the fewer and more conservative the better, especially for the more prestigious and highly sought after jobs. While body art is certainly mainstream, do not expect those whose job it is to recruit and select law enforcement applicants to be enamored with all tattoos. The exception is that standard military tattoos may help you establish rapport with someone who has served in the armed services. Facial, hand, gang and prison tattoos will have the opposite effect.

Body piercings are another area where you want to err on the conservative side. Men should avoid having any earrings during an interview while women can wear something small and business appropriate. Other body piercings are likely a real negative. Be cognizant that prior to taking a fitness tests it is standard practice to have the participants remove all jewelry to include body piercings. As a former law enforcement fitness test-administering official, I can tell you that it was annoying to wait for those persons that did not remove their jewelry prior to start of a fitness test. Even worse was having to hear complaints and whining from participants about having to take the piercings out. As far as jewelry is concerned during an interview, stick to the basics. An engagement or wedding band, college or military ring, and a nice watch are fine. Avoid friendship bracelets, cheap cosmetic jewelry and knockoff/counterfeit watches.

Regarding body odors, it is understood that American culture expects that you shower or bathe after a workout or least every 24 hours (whichever comes first). Your breath should be fresh so if you have an interview after lunch be sure to bring a toothbrush along to use prior to the face-to-face interaction. If you have chronic bad breath, get medical advice to mitigate your condition. Chewing flavored gum is OK prior to an interview, just be sure that you have properly disposed of the gum before the start of the proceedings. Discreet perfumes and colognes are a form of personal expression and pride; but overpowering scents can detract from your more important messages. Your fingernails should be kept clean and short.[104]

Like it or not an applicant's physical shape establishes an important first impression about their future work ethic, energy level, and perceived ability to perform law enforcement tasks. Again, I would like to stress this may not be objectively fair but it is certainly human nature to make assumptions based on how a person looks. Obviously, an agency fitness test will better determine an applicant's ability to perform job tasks. Changing your body shape can take many months and is a slow process. Consult your physician and fitness specialist at a gym. Do not wait for a week before a job interview. There are no shortcuts for changing your physical shape.

---

[104] http://www.fedsmith.com/article/1279/, Dress Codes, Tattoos, and Federal Employees: A Brave New World by Steve Oppermann, Thursday, June 14, 2007

Develop Interview Match Toughness

Match toughness in sports is confidence and competence from having "been there and done that." There is a very real correlation between sports match toughness and interviewing ability. In sports, the best way to develop match toughness is through real competitions. Rather than waiting to develop match toughness during the regular season, most coaches and athletes have recognized the value of preseason games.

As an example of the value of match toughness in police work: The law enforcement industry was revolutionized in the 1990s with force-on-force reality based training which is in effect an officer's preseason match. It was during the 90s that law enforcement use of force instructors universally embraced force-on-force special effects (FX) marking cartridge training. An FX marking cartridge is a paint ball that can be fired from the officer's duty weapon. Incredibly, through this reality-based training, officers typically increased their real life firearms hit rates in life or death situations from 20 percent to nearly 90 percent. Prior to the widespread use of FX marking cartridges in law enforcement training, firearms practice usually consisted of shooting at a paper silhouette and maybe using a computer simulator for judgment shooting decisions.

If all you do to prepare for a job interview is think about answers to probable interview questions then you may have the same success as an officer that has only practiced shooting his firearm at paper targets; 20 percent. Make your interview training as realistic as possible. Dress in the same clothes you will wear to an actual job interview. Have a group of three people ask you a list of questions while they sit together at one table and you are on the opposite side. Video record the practice session for your review. Ask for and accept their criticism. Do it repeatedly until you get it right. Increase your success under stress to the ninetieth percentile or better.

Location, Location, Location

There is a humorous adage the three most important aspects of property value are its location, location, and location. This can also be said of federal law enforcement jobs which interestingly also convey some "property" rights at least in the Competitive Service.

The number of applicants applying for a position is directly related to the desirability of the jobs location. The rules of supply and demand come into play. The more desirable a job location, the greater the number of applicants that will apply. Because applicants are not bidding with money for the job, there is generally an inflation in the applicant qualifications for jobs in highly sought after locations. This simply means there will be more and better competition for the job. You can improve your odds of success by applying for less sought after job locations.

Timing of Applications

I have always maintained the best time to apply for promotion is when you already have a great job. There are a couple of factors that seem to contribute to this strategy. Applicants that truly believe they already have a great job are probably performing at a superior level in their current job or at the very least are respected by their peers and supervisors. It is amazing how employment job satisfaction is directly related to self-worth. This has a huge carry over effect in confidence and competence when interviewing. Certainly, during any interview it is great to hear an applicant say they are happy and engaged in their current job. This should not be the first time you have heard that supervisors generally prefer subordinates that maintain a positive mental attitude. A positive outlook on your current job often leads to a follow up question: Why do you want to leave your current job? This is an applicant's time to lay it on thick with statements like; "Your agency has such a great reputation" or "I would like the opportunity to further develop my talents."

When it comes to promotions and the timing of job applications, there is anecdotal evidence to suggest that significant events in an applicant's life will have a positive impact on job prospects. These events could be positive such as the birth of a child or negative such as the loss of a parent or other close relative. I suspect significant life events have a positive impact because of the publicity factor: The applicant's name is being discussed and therefore on the minds of the hiring officials. Unlike Hollywood where any publicity seems to be considered good publicity, significant events involving an applicant's moral turpitude such as EEO problems will ix nay any chances for promotion.

Clean Up Your Social Media Image

We are at the dawn of the digital revolution and during this period of rapid change, there is much chaos regarding cyberspace rules of behavior. Unfortunately, many genuinely good people are doing things with the Internet and their computer they would not normally do in a public setting. There are a few recommendations for federal law enforcement job seekers with regard to this chaotic digital age and the use of social networking Web sites, e-mail addresses, and Blogs.

Background investigators routinely check for criminal history, arrests, and driving records using government databases. What you may not know is that nowadays they are also reviewing records from social networking Web sites. If you use a social networking Web site such as Facebook, Instagram, or LinkedIn be sure to portray a positive and conservative image of yourself. These Web sites are essentially public databases and are accessible by employers if they desire to find out a little more about a potential employee.

It is uncommon to find someone that does not have an e-mail address. Most people now include their e-mail address on their resume. USAJobs will even send messages to your e-mail address informing you of open vacancies that meet your defined search criteria. Vanity e-mail addresses, which are provocative, edgy, or otherwise indiscreet, should be avoided in the federal job application process. Examples would include prefixes such as hot momma or big daddy and often include numbers that have specific connotations like 666 or 69. Personally, I recommend creating a generic e-mail account through Yahoo® for the sole purpose of receiving and sending employment related e-mails.

In the early 90s there was much speculation the Internet would cause a demise of creative writing. To the contrary, the Internet has spurned a huge growth in public written expression. Many people publish material on the Internet in the form of Blogs and message threads. Again, conservatism rules the day. Written material on the Internet that is unflattering or otherwise in poor taste may not bode well with a future law enforcement employer.

Use Inter Agency/Department Agreements

Some agencies have special agreements that allow employees from one agency to apply or compete for jobs they would otherwise not be allowed to. One such agreement is the TSA/DHS agreement.

Chapter 11: After the Application and Interview – Now What?

After you have taken all the examinations and various interviews, what happens next? Well, for starters, do not expect immediate feedback unless the agency has gone to an automated system like QuickHire®. With traditional systems, a letter or e-mail will come but typically after a selection is made. This can take quite a bit of time; selections must normally be made within 120 days of the vacancy announcement closing date. If you are not selected for the position, there is an unseen benefit although not much consolation. You may get a letter or e-mail such as the example that follows.

> *Thank you for your interest in employment with the xyz agency. A final selection has been made for this position. Although, you were found to be in the best-qualified group for this position, and your name was referred to the selecting . official for consideration, you were not selected.*

This previous paragraph offers mixed blessings to the applicant. Obviously, not getting the job is the most important factor, barring that, finding out that you were highly competitive for the position is good news. If you had a selection interview, that means you now know to focus most of your efforts on improving the quality of your interview and the quality and reputation of your current work.

The letter or e-mail you do not want to get is one that states that you are **not** highly qualified for the position or even worse, you did not meet the minimum qualification for the position. If this is the situation you find yourself in, then you totally wasted your time, money, and effort applying for that job. You have a few options:
- Find a less prestigious job to apply for
- Improve you basic qualifications (education and experience)
- Improve your examination scores (rewrite the KSAs, practice the written tests, get better quality specialized experience)
- Find a noncompetitive method for selection and convince the selecting official to hire you.

One thing is for certain, if you keep doing the same thing, you are likely to get the same results. Making real improvements in life to get the things you really want almost always involves a series of small steps. Are you willing to do what it takes to get the job? You may want to review the previous chapter for suggestions.

Many books and job hunting experts recommend the applicant send thank you letters to your interview officials after going through an interview. These letters probably work better in the real world but not so much in the realm of law enforcement. I am not saying it is never done. I have received a few of them although none ever came from an applicant that I recommended for a job. If you feel compelled to write a thank you letter, ensure the accuracy of the name, job titles, spelling, and grammar. An article in FedSmith.com, whose target audience is all federal employees, recommends sending a thank you letter after an interview. I highly respect their opinion as you may note the large number of times I have cited their Web page articles. However, I would still argue the point: The always pragmatic, often cynical, and mostly testosterone driven law enforcement side of the federal government really does not care or expect a thank you letter.

The Job Offer

If you are selected for a position, you can expect a phone call where the caller will verbally offer you the job by asking if you are still willing to accept the position. "Yes", should be your only response unless you have just won the lottery or have already been given a better job offer. If you decline, the position there will be no second offers for that job. In the event that you are expecting another federal job offer, do not worry because accepting the first offer does not disqualify you from others. Law enforcement job offers are usually conditional on passing a medical, drug, and background screening process. Some agencies are doing these screening processes prior to the final job offer. Those offered career advancement or lateral transfers might already have the conditional boxes checked off so they immediately proceed to the next step. Remember, selected does not mean appointed.

After passing all of the conditional requirements, an enter on duty date (EOD) is established. To do this, the newly selected applicant and the hiring agency enter into discussions regarding the date that suits both parties. If the federal government currently employs the selected person, that agency/office is primarily involved in these discussions rather than the selected employee. The agency/office getting the new employee is often referred to as the gaining office while the agency/office losing the employee is referred to as the losing office. The gaining office usually wants to have the new employee working for their office sooner rather than later and the losing office usually takes the opposite position. The bottom line is you can expect at least a two-week transition period but usually not much more than a month. EOD dates typically are on the first day of a two-week federal pay period.

Federal agencies do have authority to pay move money, house hunting trips, hiring bonuses and other financial incentives. These incentives are based on previous federal employment and are usually never available for entry-level positions. Incentives are typically used in higher paid positions and for jobs that are difficult to fill. Regarding the pay grade that is offered, there is usually not much input from the new employee. The rules on pay are pre-established. Although with the advent of Pay Banding systems such as that used by TSA, there is some latitude on the part of the agency. In the GS system, the largest pay system for the federal government, new employees are usually given the lowest advertised grade that was offered in the vacancy unless there is prior federal experience. They are given a step within that grade which provides slightly more money than their previous federal employment. See the chapter regarding Federal Salaries for more information on this. Agencies that have a pay banding system have more latitude on starting salaries.

Depending upon a number of factors, new employees will likely serve in a probationary period. This is usually one year but usually less than two. The probationary period limits legal and administrative recourse should an Agency wish to terminate a probationary employee. Employees that have already served a similar probationary period with another federal agency are usually exempt from this new probationary period. Excepted Service employees do not have much in the way of recourse anyhow so probationary periods are somewhat meaningless. The probationary period is your opportunity to start fresh and make a great impression. New employees should show up to work at a minimum of fifteen minutes before the start of the pay clock. This includes all of the time when you are in training such as at the Federal Law Enforcement Training Center, FBI/DEA Academy in Quantico, or any other training facility.

As a first line law enforcement Supervisor, I can tell you the top things your immediate Supervisor expects is that you show up to work on time, and don't abuse sick leave. While at work, have a positive mental attitude. Be the reserved optimist rather than the office pessimist. I hope that your new agency has a mentoring program. If not, find someone that will assist you until you get familiar with the work routine and performance/conduct expectations.

It seems natural amongst many law enforcement types to be cynical regarding some facets of their life. While this may be necessary demeanor while investigating crimes it provides no benefit while applying or awaiting to hear about a job. Cynical job seekers usually have the attitude and make statements that someone has been preselected for the position; there is a good-old-boys club, or any host of other reasons why they will not get the job.

Words of caution: A hiring official does not want to hear cynics whine about a job announcement. If you truly believe there is an unscrupulous conspiracy against you, check the list of prohibited personnel, actions listed later in this chapter and take appropriate action. While awaiting to hear if you have been selected for a job, try to do your best at your current job. Background investigators or hiring officials may be calling your current employer at that very moment to get a job reference recommendation.

Don't Put Your House Up For Sale

After an interview and in anticipation of getting your new job, do not put your house up for sale. There are a couple of reasons why you should not do this. The appearance to other applicants is that you were selected in advance and the fix was in place. Things can change quickly; your name may never clear the background checks. Someone may file a grievance or legal action and in effect freeze the position before you are appointed.

Another reason for not jumping the gun is financial related. The government does on occasion do a housing buyout, essentially a purchase of the employee's house. If you put your house on the market before you actually are officially offered the position, you may disqualify yourself from the buyout program. Many people who are confident of getting the job offer do use their time wisely and prepare their house and other areas of their life for the probable change.

While the previous thoughts on this topic are about literally selling your house, the words also apply figuratively. Do not burn any bridges and take this opportune moment to tell your employer what you "really" think. Do not brag to your coworkers about how much money you are going to be making. I also recommend not telling relatives and others that you are getting a new job until you actually have the job offer. I have made this mistake at least once and it leads to some lengthy explanations if the job falls though even if it is of no fault of your own.

Prohibited Personnel Practices

If you think you have been the victim of an unfair action with regard to your job application, you may want to read the following. There are twelve prohibited personnel practices in the Executive Branch (Not the FBI, CIA, or NSA). These prohibited practices include reprisal for whistleblowing, and are defined by law at § 2302(b) of title 5 of the United States Code (U.S.C.). A personnel action (such as an appointment, promotion, reassignment, or suspension) may need to be involved for a prohibited personnel practice to occur. Generally stated, § 2302(b) provides that a federal employee authorized to take, direct others to take, recommend or approve any personnel action may not:

1. discriminate against an employee or applicant based on race, color, religion, sex, national origin, age, handicapping condition, marital status, or political affiliation;
2. solicit or consider employment recommendations based on factors other than personal knowledge or records of job related abilities or characteristics;
3. coerce the political activity of any person;
4. deceive or willfully obstruct anyone from competing for employment;
5. influence anyone to withdraw from competition for any position so as to improve or injure the employment prospects of any other person;
6. give an unauthorized preference or advantage to anyone so as to improve or injure the employment prospects of any particular employee or applicant;
7. engage in nepotism (i.e., hire, promote, or advocate the hiring or promotion of relatives);
8. engage in reprisal for whistleblowing – i.e., take, fail to take, or threaten to take or fail to take a personnel action with respect to any employee or applicant because of any disclosure of information by the employee or applicant that he or she reasonably believes evidences a violation of a law, rule or regulation; gross mismanagement; gross waste of funds; an abuse of authority; or a substantial and specific danger to public health or safety (if such disclosure is not barred by law and such information is not specifically required by Executive Order to be kept secret in the interest of national defense or the conduct of foreign affairs – if so restricted by law or Executive Order, the disclosure is only protected if made to the Special Counsel, the Inspector General, or comparable agency official);
9. take, fail to take, or threaten to take or fail to take a personnel action against an employee or applicant for exercising an appeal, complaint, or grievance right; testifying for or assisting another in exercising such a right; cooperating with or disclosing information to the Special Counsel or to an Inspector General; or refusing to obey an order that would require the individual to violate a law;
10. discriminate based on personal conduct which is not adverse to the on-the-job performance of an employee, applicant, or others; or
11. take or fail to take, recommend, or approve a personnel action if taking or failing to take such an action would violate a veterans' preference requirement; and
12. take or fail to take a personnel action, if taking or failing to take action would violate any law, rule or regulation implementing or directly concerning merit system principles at 5 U.S.C. § 2301.

One of the biggest mistakes a federal job interviewer can unwittingly make is to ask a job applicant about their family, medical conditions/health, or religion. For example: An interviewing official asks a single parent applicant how he or she intends to raise their children while being away from home so much with a law enforcement job. Questions or dialog that touches on such topics is irrelevant for the hiring process even if they are done with the best of intentions or just to make conversation. If you think you have been the victim of a prohibited personnel practice, you may contact the Office of Special Counsel.

The Negative Response

It may take weeks or even months, but eventually you will find out the decision regarding your job application. If you were not offered a job, a public outcry displaying your displeasure is not going to help. If this was a Merit Promotion (career advancement) job, the worst thing you can do is to have a sour attitude. If you need emotional support, seek it at home. Within the law enforcement circles, word will travel fast about such behavior. The best thing I did after not getting a job promotion was to happily go about my business. I even told others that I was glad for the person that got job I had wanted. Was I sincere? Hell no! I was better qualified and should have gotten the job. I have since proven that with the quality of my work. However, my positive attitude after not getting the first promotion was noticed by at least one person that was a peer of the hiring officials. He even went so far as to indicate that my positive attitude would be beneficial next time around. On the next job announcement, I got the promotion. On a few occasions, persons I have supervised have acted childish after their nonselection for a promotion. Their behavior had a lasting impact on my view of them. Enough said.

Turning down a Job Offer

Every occasionally a selected applicant will receive a job offer and turn down the position. I suppose there are a number of reasons for this. Maybe the person had second thoughts on the duty location, maybe family or health reasons necessitated the change of heart. One thing is, do not ever expect to get another job offer from an agency after turning them down. It is possible that in another location with the same agency a different hiring official is unaware of your previous flip-flop decision and decides to hire you. Possible but not probable. It will probably come out in the interview or background investigation that you had been offered a job before. The problem is the indecisiveness issue and the fact the recommending official looked foolish for suggesting your name in the first place and then had to go back and do more paperwork to get a name to replace yours.

There are of course legitimate reasons for turning down a job offer and the choice is yours. I have been on both sides of this issue, as the applicant and as the recommending official. I once made a bad decision when I turned down a Deputy Marshals job in a choice location. I have had applicants turn down jobs after spending countless hours going through interviews and convincing the selecting official that our recommended applicants were solid. When the selected applicant withdrew, it did not sit well with my boss.

A Few Last Words

I have known many people that hold their GS grade level as an important measuring tool of their self-worth/self-esteem. I have always held the belief that your GS grade or job title is the last thing that should count in this regard. Personally, I do not have much respect for a person that confirms their self-worth through their job title. They are saying, "I am better than you because I make more money." There are many people better than me that for one reason or another have managed to stay at the lower end of the GS Scale. There are also many Senior Executives that do not quite measure up to par in the values and ethics category. I have had one or two bosses in this category and the former New York Governor Spitzer is an image that comes to mind.

These few last words are intended to pass along some insightful thoughts for persons that do not attain a job for which they have applied. Keep your head held high. Focus on improving your resume by getting more and better experience. Use the many techniques, tactics, and strategies written in this Chapter to increase your odds of success.

Chapter 12: Lessons Learned - True Stories from Job Applicants

Example #1:

In the spring of 1991, I went to a job interview for a Deputy Marshals position. As I remember, I had applied for an All Sources Vacancy Announcement and it the job location was for Burlington, VT. It really was a dream job at a great location. There were a few strange occurrences during that interview adventure that I look back upon and laugh. I remember being called to set up a time for the face-to-face interview. Having friends in Burlington, I was fortunate to be able to visit with them and do the business of the interview.

I flew to Burlington from Toronto where I was working for the United States Customs Service. I flew out on a Friday and was returning on a Sunday. The interview was Saturday morning at 8:00 at the Federal Building. I got all dressed up in my best (only) interview suit. My friend that I am staying with drops me off and I plan to meet him back at the same location in two hours. I wait outside the Federal Building so as not to be too early.

At about 20 minutes prior to my scheduled time, I go to the Marshals office only to be informed the location had changed to a hotel near the Burlington Airport. The secretary informed me they had called my home phone on Friday and left this information on my answering machine. She calls the hotel and advises her boss that I would be arriving soon. No car and wearing suit I exit the building and go the main street, which was surprisingly empty. I started hitchhiking to the new location about three miles away. Got a ride right away and make it to the right place. I meet the supervisor who asks if I am ready.

I am the first one to be interviewed, about a 40-minute process. The interview room is a suite in the hotel with the beds removed and in its place, a long table with four chairs behind it. There is one chair about six feet in front of the table and I was told to have a seat in that chair. I remember trying to bring the chair closer to the table as it seemed a little awkward to be sitting in the middle of a room by oneself. Immediately I am corrected and told to put the chair back and have a seat in the chair. I figured out in a short time that this was meant to be a stress interview.

Interestingly, one of the persons in the interview room appeared to be dozing off in the sofa that was slightly behind and to the left of me. To this day, I do not know if that was a set up looking for a reaction by me or if the person was really that tired that he needed sleep at eight in the morning. The interview went well. I do distinctly recall them asking a couple questions about my fitness award I had received when I went through the Customs Inspector training.

The fitness test I took when I got the award is the same test given to all law enforcement basic students including deputy Marshals. After the interview questions were completed, the Supervisor had me go into another room where he asked that I complete some other paperwork. This would be my first clue that I had gotten the job. In fact, I had completed the paperwork correctly in advance but the Supervisor said that I left something out. I filled in the apparently missing information; I think it wanted a passport number although upon reviewing the instructions I was not supposed to put it in. I did not question the person's orders and filled in the information. About a month goes by and I get a call asking me if I will accept the position and be at the Marshals academy in a two weeks. I accept. I take my drug test and pass. I see the apartment manager about getting out of my lease. They tell me I cannot start having second thoughts.

Example #2:
The setting: A young physically fit, college educated man had his second and likely final interview with the Department of State as he was in the final process for being hired as a Special Agent in their Diplomatic Security Service. Two Special Agents from DOS showed up for this interview with the prospective employee. The man being interviewed had excellent recommendations from his current federal supervisor and he had a rabbi who had made some phone calls for him. The interview question that blew it for him was simple. Question: As a DOS Special Agent, you are expected to help spread the word on why the United States is a great democracy. What are your thoughts on this?

Answer: Any idiot knows the United States is a representative republic and not a democracy. Unfortunately, you can be 100 percent correct in your answer but also be dead wrong. His career prospects, including GS 13 pay, twenty-year retirement, overseas job postings, overseas housing allowances were all kissed goodbye with this one answer. It is not that the prospective employee's answer was wrong, in fact, he was right.

However, no one likes a smart aleck. No one likes to shown their question was in err. No one wants a troublemaker. It was an important lesson to learn. Too bad this prospective employee did not think out his answer a little better. Could have said something like, it is great to live in a country where the Constitution, the three branches of federal government, and free elections have enabled persons from any socioeconomic background to become president or to fulfill their dream of being a law enforcement officer with the DOS.

Example #3:
Two freshmen college students get SCEP positions with the Bureau of Land Management (BLM). The BLM pays for college tuition and a salary for the two to go to college and work part-time during the school semester and full-time during the summer. The first student keeps her grades up, works hard, and is hired as a law enforcement park ranger upon graduation from college. The second student gets two years of school paid for before being fired for not keeping her grades up and lying about having credit card problems.

Chapter 13: Becoming a Park Ranger

So, you want to be a park ranger. You have selected one of the top ten dream jobs in the United States. Let us talk about the different kinds of park rangers. There are three different types of park rangers. There are law enforcement park rangers, interpretive park rangers, and backcountry rangers. The National Park Service call them law enforcement ranger, interpretive rangers, and general rangers. In the federal government job series, park rangers are the 0025 job series.

National Park Service seasonal law enforcement park rangers attend training at one of the seven seasonal park ranger law enforcement academies or at the Federal Law Enforcement Training Center in Glynco, Georgia. Both present a 17-week land management police training program comprised of physical fitness, firearms, driving, defensive tactics, and lectured-based classes. Full time law enforcement park rangers received a police retirement known as a "6-C" retirement, allowing them to retire at age 50 or at 25 years of service. Seasonal rangers do not receive a 6-C retirement.

Attending a seasonal ranger academy is something you sign up for and you pay for. Attending the Federal Law Enforcement Training Center is something an agency pays for once you have been hired. If an agency has hired you, that is based on your possessing experience either as a military veteran, local police officer, or as a seasonal ranger. It costs the government approximately $50,000 per student to attend the Land Management Police Training Program, so they generally do not hire someone right out of college. This is especially true when park ranger is at the top of many of people's dream job lists.

The seasonal park ranger law enforcement academies are 720 hours of training offered at the following locations: Skagit Valley College in Mount Vernon, Washington, Southwestern Community College in Franklin, North Carolina, Temple University in Philadelphia, Pennsylvania, Vermilion Community College in Ely, Minnesota, Colorado Northwestern Community College in Rangeley, Colorado, Northern Arizona University in Flagstaff, Arizona, and Santa Rosa Junior College in Windsor, California. Each college utilizes the same National Park Service curriculum.

Some of the seasonal ranger academies such as Vermilion Community College offer dual certifications, allowing certification both as a National Park Service seasonal ranger and once you take the Minnesota Police Officer Standards of Training test, you are Minnesota POST certified. Post certification allows access to any state, county, or city police, conservation officer, or park ranger job in Minnesota. That expands your hiring potential exponentially. You can go to any state POST website and examine law enforcement jobs in that state. Some states are having a hard time filling game warden positions, state police, and police jobs.

The challenge with park ranger jobs is limiting yourself to one state or one park. For example, the student who says that they are only willing to live and work in their home state. This negates many opportunities in other states, parks, and areas. A park ranger goes where the work is. I worked in Gateway National Recreation Area, Golden Gateway

National Recreation Area, and many others. Each move was a promotional opportunity, but each move came with personal challenges for my family. Some moves were paid for and some I paid for. Many a park ranger will tell you that you will be paid in sunsets.

Some of the urban parks are status parks, meaning you can transition from seasonal to full time park ranger easier than most parks because of the need there. Therefore, you can attain full time status in record time. Other candidates have achieved status by becoming dispatchers, working in maintenance, or taking a non-ranger job they did not want to until a fulltime law enforcement ranger job opened up. The competition for park ranger jobs in the National Park Service is incredibly high. Rangers do not retire until they hit mandatory retirement at 57 years of age. That sounds like it is a long way off, but it catches up with you very quick.

Most full time law enforcement park rangers began their careers as seasonal law enforcement park rangers. Park rangers usually work a summer or two as a seasonal ranger before getting on full time. These seasonal jobs are their proving ground. It is their chance to shine and show a chief ranger all that they can accomplish. In the off-season, these seasonal rangers work as ski patrol, back country guides, or other outdoor industry jobs. Some seasonal rangers prefer the seasonal life and the freedom and variety it represents to them. Some rangers get their start in internships such as the Student Conservation Association or AmeriCorps.

The second kind of park ranger are interpretive park rangers. These rangers are generalists and tend to have training in history and interpretation similar to a docent. Some interpretive rangers work as period role players wearing historic costumes depending on the park location and specific history. One of my old supervisors was a historic role player in Williamsburg, Virginia wearing period costume and driving a horse wagon around town talking to tourists. Interpretive rangers give lectures of their respective park, while some build and create displays.

Backcountry rangers or general rangers can provide a variety of duties from trail maintenance to performing generalist duties designed to facilitate visitor understanding of the park. This could mean operating a fee collection booth, resource conservation, or public use management as deemed by the park superintendent. I worked with a seasonal backcountry ranger who was an emergency medical technician, who patrolled the backcountry of Yosemite National Park rescuing lost hikers, treating bruised feet, and being paid to backpack the Sierras. In the off-season, he worked for the National Outdoor Leadership School teaching classes.

The National Park Service hires approximately 10,000 seasonal employees annually to provide visitor services during peak summer visitation. The Park Service's current workforce includes approximately permanent 27,000 full time employees. The variety of positions include campground rangers, fee collectors, tour guides, naturalists, biological technicians, landscape architects, firefighters, laborers, law enforcement rangers, lifeguards, clerk typists, carpenters, and historians.
The National Park Service Seasonal Rangers work for 1,039 hours annually that is just

under 26 weeks or six months. For most parks, that is June-August. A seasonal ranger can go back to the same park each year, or bounce from park to park and travel the country. Seasonal rangers can work during the winter if that is a period of heavy visitation. That is rare, but can happen. The National Park Service also has special agents.

Now, let us talk about other park ranger agencies. There is the Fish & Wildlife Service. They have special agents, law enforcement rangers called refuge officers, and wildlife inspectors. They also have interpretive rangers called outreach or education specialists that do the job of an interpretive ranger and more. With Fish & Wildlife, they are a biology-based agency. So, biologists rule. You do not need a biology background, but it does not hurt.

The Fish & Wildlife Service have their own 533-acre training facility called the National Conservation Training Center in Shepherdstown, West Virginia. The Fish & Wildlife Service have their own wildlife forensic wildlife crime lab in Ashland, Oregon. The crime lab employs forensic scientists.

Fish & Wildlife Service special agents attend the 12-week Criminal Investigator Training Program and their agency specific add-on Special Agent Basic School. Graduates then attend the field training evaluation program. Refuge Officers enjoy a similar regime with attending the 17-week Land management Police Training Program before attending their add-on Refuge Officer Basic School and then the 12-week field training evaluation program.

Fish & Wildlife Service officers and agents will spend a large amount of time learning bird identification. The agency will train you to become an expert in birds. Wildlife Inspectors attend the eight-week Wildlife Inspector Basic School at the Federal Law Enforcement Training Center. A wildlife inspector is an unarmed uniformed officer who works at major airports and ports of entry working alongside Customs & Border Protection looking for wildlife and wildlife parts smugglers.

The Fish & Wildlife Service has seasonal park rangers such as a fee collector at Chincoteague National Wildlife Refuge, who works the summer months controlling access to the refuge in a fee collection booth.

The Forest Service is another agency with park rangers. The US Forest Service has special agents, law enforcement park rangers called officers, forest protection officers and they have seasonal interpretive park rangers. A forest protection officer can write tickets, but it unarmed. The Forest Service tends to have more firefighter and fire technician jobs than park rangers jobs. The Forest Service is funny about differentiating themselves from the National Park Service, hence their uniformed rangers being called officers.

The Forest Service have line authority. This means a law enforcement officer works for a law enforcement supervisor, who works for a patrol captain, who works for a patrol commander. Both the National Park Service and the Fish & Wildlife Service do not have line authority in their uniformed rangers, so law enforcement works for non-law enforcement. Working for non-law enforcement has challenges, as law enforcement is expensive and takes away from other divisions.

Another park ranger based agency is the Army Corps of Engineers. These uniformed rangers are non-law enforcement who manage and patrol army corps recreational facilities peppered around the US. Army Corps rangers manage campgrounds and park facilities, write tickets and carry pepper spray, but are unarmed.

All fifty states have state park rangers, in addition to county, and city park rangers. Most states have uniformed conservations officers or game wardens. Some states possess park ranger training academies and some do not. All are uniformed and tend to be separated into law enforcement and non-law enforcement. Many attend the local state or county police academy alongside the uniformed police. Many of the state and local parks also have seasonal ranger positions that they employ during the summer only.

Lastly, I would be remiss if I did not mention the National Marine Fisheries Service. The National Marine Fisheries Service protect fish populations, threatened marine species and fish habitats. They have special agent and uniform officers who enforce fish laws and protect marine species. They are not park rangers, but they have a conservation-based mission. They spend a lot of their time on the water, so you will learn to operate boats of varying sizes.

Two additional agencies that are not park ranger-based but have a similar mission are worth talking about. The US Park Police are the full-time urban uniformed police of the National Park Service. They work in Washington DC, New York City, and San Francisco. The US Park Police attend the 12-week Uniformed Police Training Program at the Federal Law Enforcement Training Center before attending agency specific add-on training and then participating in the 12-week field training evaluation program.

The US Park Police have uniformed patrol, plainclothes criminal investigators, and a variety of specialty units. These include the horse mounted patrol unit, marine boat unit, the motorcycle unit, and the special weapons and tactics team. Bike units, canine officers, and the aviation unit round out the field units. The Park Police also have a training branch that manages all of their training basic, advanced, and in-service training.

The other agency is the Tennessee Valley Authority (TVA) Police. The TVA Police are like the National Marine Fisheries Service in that they are small but mighty. The TVA Police patrol the recreation areas of the Tennessee Valley Authority in Alabama, Georgia, Kentucky, Mississippi, North Carolina, Tennessee, and Virginia. Originally, there were a uniformed police, but their role has transitioned to more of a combination of inspector, investigator, and security role in an around the power facilities of the Tennessee Valley Authority.

All 50 states have state park rangers with varying levels of training. Some have seasonal rangers like the National Park Service based on the seasonal visitation that most parks experience. Some counties and cities have park rangers, also. Some of the state, county, and local law enforcement rangers attend training at their local policy academy, whether at the state or county level. Some ranger agencies have their own training academies such as the state of Florida.

Park ranger jobs require an associate degree at a minimum, and a bachelor is the preferred degree for candidates. The degree can be in law enforcement, biology, history, or any other field. The four-year degree shows your well roundedness and that you can complete something you started. The difference between the two and four year degrees is your starting salary. More college means more money to start. A master degree helps once you get into management. A doctorate will help if you go into training.

Some closing thoughts on becoming a park ranger. Rangers tend to work alone. Backup is usually further away than you think. You must be able to think on your feet, be independent, and resilient. Do not complain, always have a smile, and volunteer every chance you get to help. Avoid local politics and do not badmouth anybody on the staff no matter how much you do not like them. The person you badmouth has wives, husbands, and associates that work for the Park Service. Being a role model is how you stand out and make a chief ranger remember whom you are and thus they will want to invite you back again the following summer.

Chapter 14 Glossary of Terms

Ability	A competence to perform an observable behavior or a behavior that results in an observable product.
Administrative Law Judge (ALJ)	An independent, impartial trier of fact in formal administrative hearings. An ALJ is similar to that of a trial judge conducting civil trials without a jury. In general, ALJs prepare for and preside at formal hearings required by statute, to be held under or in substantial accord with provisions of the Administrative Procedure Act, in sections 553-559 of title 5, United States Code (5 U.S.C. §553, 5 U.S.C. §554, 5 U.S.C. §555, 5 U.S.C. §556, 5 U.S.C. §557, 5 U.S.C. §558, 5 U.S.C. §559)
Agency Certification Program	A certification developed by an agency, group of agencies, or other group that demonstrates a person's proficiency in the job-related competencies/KSAs. An agency certification program does not have to be recognized by a professional community.
Applicant	A person who applies for a vacant position.
Appointee	The person who is ultimately appointed to a position, and who enters on board with the hiring agency.
Appointing Officer	A person having the authority, by law, or by duly delegated authority, to appoint, employ, or promote individuals to positions in an agency.
Appointing Authority	The legal or regulatory basis on which a specific appointment may be made to a Federal civilian position.

Office of Personnel Management 1900 E Street NW, Washington, DC 20415 | (202) 606-1800 | TTY (202) 606-2532

Adjusted Career Earnings--A figure based on an employee's earnings history that is used in calculating Social Security benefits amounts. A worker's actual earnings throughout his or her work history are indexed to reflect the national wage levels in effect when he/she becomes eligible for Social Security benefits.

Agency Automatic (1%) Contribution--An amount equal to 1% of a FERS employee's basic pay that his or her agency contributes to the employee's Thrift Savings Plan account each pay period. This contribution is made from agency funds; it is not a deduction from the employee's basic pay. It is made whether or not the employee contributes to the Thrift Savings Plan.

Agency Matching Contributions--A FERS employee who contributes a percentage of his or her pay to the Thrift Savings Plan receives additional contributions from the Government. These Government contributions are known as Agency Matching Contributions.

Annuitant--An individual who is receiving a CSRS, CSRS-Offset or FERS annuity.

Annuity--The recurring monthly payments to a former employee who has retired.

Annuity, Deferred--An annuity that begins more than 1 month after separation from employment at some future point when retirement age is reached. (Also called deferred benefits.)

Annuity, Immediate--An annuity that becomes payable within 1 month after separation from federal employment. (Also called immediate benefits.)

Annuity, Postponed--Delaying your FERS annuity benefit to sometime in the future after meeting your Minimum Retirement Age but before age 62.

Annuity, Reduced--A retiree's basic annuity that is reduced because of retirement before a certain age (for reasons other than disability). Annuities are also reduced because of unpaid deposits or redeposits, or to provide a survivor annuity. (Also called reduced benefits.)

Annuity, Survivor--The recurring monthly payments to a deceased employee or retiree's survivor(s). Survivor annuities may be paid to surviving spouses, certain former spouses, and children. (Also called survivor benefits.)

Average Indexed Monthly Earnings (AIME)--The adjusted earnings determined under the Social Security Act formula used to determine Social Security benefits. It is based on an individual's lifetime earnings subject to the Social Security System.

Basic Benefit Plan--The first tier of FERS (Federal Employees Retirement System). The Basic Benefit Plan provides annuities and lump-sum payments based on years of service and pay.

Basic Pay--An employee's pay subject to retirement deductions under CSRS or the FERS Basic Benefit Plan, generally excluding such compensation as bonuses, overtime pay, special allowances, etc.

COLA, CSRS--CSRS cost of living adjustments (COLA's) provide an increase that is equal to the rate of inflation as measured by the Consumer Price Index (CPI). CSRS cost-of-living-adjustments are provided to retirees at all ages.

COLA, FERS--FERS cost of living adjustments (COLA's) provide an increase that is equal to the rate of inflation as measured by the Consumer Price Index (CPI) when the inflation rate is 2% or less. When the inflation rate is between 2% and 3%, the cost-of-living-adjustments will be 2%. When the inflation rate is 3% or more, FERS cost-of-living-adjustments are 1% less than the rate of inflation. FERS cost-of-living-adjustments under the Basic Benefit Plan are not provided until a retiree reaches age 62, except for disability and survivor benefits, and employees retired under the special provisions for law enforcement officers, firefighter, and air traffic controllers.

Common Stock Index Investment Fund (C Fund)--One of the three Thrift Savings Plan investment funds. This fund allows participants to invest in common stocks and is invested in a fund that tracks the Standard and Poor's 500 stock index.

Consumer Price Index (CPI)--The measure of change in consumer prices as determined by a monthly survey of the Bureau of Labor Statistics. Among the Consumer Price Index components are the costs of housing, food, transportation, and electricity. Both CSRS and FERS benefits are adjusted for changes in the rate of inflation as measured by the Consumer Price Index. (See Cost-of-living-adjustments entries.)

Cost-of-Living Adjustment (COLA)--An adjustment of an annuity amount based on the rate of inflation as measured by the Consumer Price Index (CPI). It protects an annuity's buying power in times of inflation.

Credits of Coverage -A measurement used to credit work covered by Social Security. In 1998, earnings totaling $700 generally equal one credit of coverage. No more than four credits may be earned in any one calendar year. The term "quarters" of coverage is also used.

CSRS--The Civil Service Retirement System.

CSRS Offset--Generally applies to an employee who was originally employed under CSRS, left the federal service for more than a year, and returned after 1983 to be covered by both CSRS and Social Security. If you elect FERS, CSRS-Offset service changes to FERS service.

Deductions--The amount withheld from the basic pay of an employee for the basic retirement benefit plan.

Deposit--A sum of money paid into CSRS or FERS by an employee (or a survivor) to get credit for a period of federal civilian service during which retirement deductions were not withheld from pay.

Earnings Offset--A reduction in an employee's Social Security payments or Special Retirement Supplement made when he/she continues to work after benefits begin and earns over an allowable amount ($9,120 in 1998). For every $2 earned over this amount, the employee will give up $1 in benefits. This offset does not apply to special groups of employees until the Minimum Retirement Age is attained.

Earnings Test--A method of connecting benefits to income so that as income increases, benefits decrease. Used in the earnings offset.

FERS--The Federal Employees Retirement System.

Federal Retirement Thrift Investment Board--An independent Federal agency established to administer the Thrift Savings Plan.

Fixed Income Investment Fund (F Fund)--One of the three Thrift Savings Plan investment funds. This fund allows participants to invest in fixed income obligations and is invested in a fund designed to closely track the Lehman Brothers Aggregate bond index.

Government Pension Offset--A part of the Social Security law that affects CSRS retirees who are also entitled to a Social Security spouse or survivor benefit. It is sometimes referred to as the "Public Pension Offset." The Social Security benefit is reduced because the CSRS retiree is also receiving a pension from employment that was not covered by Social Security. If you elect FERS, you must be covered for 5 years to avoid Government Pension Offset.

Government Securities Investment Fund (G Fund)--One of the three Thrift Savings plan investment funds. This fund consists exclusively of investments in short-term nonmarketable Treasury securities specially issued to the TSP.

High-3 Average Pay--The average of an employee's 3 highest consecutive years of basic pay earned during creditable service. Used in benefit computations under both FERS and CSRS.

Market Rate of Interest--The percentage of interest paid on certain FERS deposits and refunds. Based on the average interest earned by the Civil Service Retirement and Disability Fund in the previous year. In 1998, the interest rate is 6.75%.

Maximum Taxable Wage Base--The maximum amount of an employee's wages subject to Social Security taxes. In 1997, the maximum taxable wage base is $68,400. An employee pays no Social Security taxes on any earnings above the base. However, the excess earnings are not used in calculating the Social Security benefit, either. The maximum taxable wage base increases yearly based on the average increase in earnings of the American workforce as a whole.

Minimum Retirement Age (MRA)--The earliest age at which a FERS employee may retire voluntarily or elect to receive benefits if separated from federal service after at least 10 years of service. The MRA varies according to the year in which the employee was born. For anyone born before 1948, the MRA is 55. It increases gradually to 57 for those born later. The benefits of an employee who has less than 30 years of service (or who is not age 60 with 20 years of service) are reduced it he/she elects to receive them at the MRA.

Non-CSRS Offset Service--Civilian service performed before the effective date of a transfer to FERS that was not subject to both CSRS and Social Security deductions. Non-CSRS Offset service includes nondeduction service performed before transferring to FERS, service for which a deposit or redeposit has been made at the full CSRS rate, and service for which deductions were taken at the full CSRS rate, whether refunded or not.

OASDI or Social Security Tax--The part of the Social Security tax that goes to the old age, survivor, and disability insurance. Since 1990, the tax rate has been 6.2% up to the maximum taxable wage base. The total Social Security tax also includes 1.45% for Medicare.

Offset Plan--(See CSRS Offset.)

OPM (Office of Personnel Management)--The Federal Government's central personnel agency. OPM administers the CSRS and the FERS Basic Benefit Plan.

Primary Insurance Amount--A worker's basic Social Security benefit based on his or her adjusted career earnings. (See Adjusted Career Earnings.)

Quarters of Coverage ("Quarters")--A measurement used to credit work covered by Social Security. In 1998, earnings totaling $700 generally equal one quarter of coverage. No more than four quarters of coverage may be earned in any one calendar year. The term **"credit"** is also used to refer to quarters of coverage.

Reasonable Offer--For discontinued service retirement (early, involuntary), a reasonable offer is a written offer of another position in the employing agency for which an individual is qualified, not lower than two grades below the individual's current grade, at the same tenure and work schedule, and in the same commuting area. A different definition applies for disability retirement: A written offer of another position in the employing agency for which an individual is qualified, at the same grade as the individual's current grade, at the same tenure and work schedule, and in the same commuting area.

Redeposit--A sum of money paid into CSRS by an employee (or a survivor) to get credit for a period of federal civilian service for which a refund of retirement contributions was received. (Not allowable for FERS service.))

Refund--The amount of money a former federal employee withdraws from his or her retirement account. Under FERS, refunds are paid with a market rate of interest.

Retiree--A former federal employee who is receiving recurring CSRS or FERS payments based on his or her service.

Retirement, Deferred--Retirement under CSRS or FERS when the employee separates from service with at least 5 years of civilian service, but before meeting the requirements for an immediate annuity. A deferred retirement under CSRS begins on the employee's 62nd birthday. Under FERS, the deferred retirement can begin as early as the employee's MRA if the employee had at least 10 years of service.

Retirement, Early, FERS--Retirement with at least 10 but less than 30 years of service after reaching the MRA and receiving a reduced annuity. Not available under CSRS. Also called "MRA + 10" benefit.

Retirement Fund--The Civil Service Retirement and Disability Fund. This is the account that contains the employee and employer contributions to CSRS and FERS. It includes additional payments, as well, and is invested in federal government securities.

Retirement, Unreduced--Retirement under CSRS or FERS with full benefits after meeting appropriate age and length-of-service requirements: 62 with 5 years, 60 with 20 years, 55 with 30 years under CSRS, or the MRA with 30 years or involuntary and early out under FERS. (Also called unreduced benefits.)

Retirement, Voluntary, or Optional--Retirement from federal service under CSRS or FERS at the individual's option with an immediate annuity at any time following completion of the appropriate age and length-of-service requirements.

Service, Nondeduction--Periods of civilian service for which no retirement deductions were withheld from pay for retirement purposes.

Social Security--A social insurance program that covers most of the Nation's work force. It is often the basic retirement plan to which other benefits are added. It provides retirement, disability, survivor, and Medicare benefits.

Social Security Credits--When an employee works in a position and pays Social Security taxes, he/she earns Social Security credits. Minimum numbers of credits are required in order to qualify for various Social Security benefits. (See Quarters of Coverage.)

Special Retirement Supplement--An annuity supplement provided to some FERS employees who retire before age 62, because Social Security benefits cannot start before then. The supplement approximates the portion of a full career Social Security benefit earned while under FERS, and ends at age 62 when Social Security benefits first become available. The supplement is subject to an earnings test.

Substantial Social Security Coverage or Earnings--Earnings above a certain amount that count toward reducing the effect of the Windfall Elimination Provision (WEP). The effect of the WEP starts to be reduced when 21 or more years of substantial Social Security coverage are earned. (In 1998, $12,675 in earnings subject to Social Security taxes are considered to be "substantial." In contrast, the amount needed to earn four credits for the year is $2,875.) (See Windfall Elimination Provision.)

Survivor--A person who is entitled to a benefit based on the service of a deceased employee or annuitant.

Thrift Savings Plan (TSP)--A retirement savings and investment plan established by Congress in the Federal Employees' Retirement System Act of 1986 to provide eligible federal employees savings and tax benefits similar to those offered by many private corporations. It is a defined contribution plan administered by the Federal Retirement Thrift Investment Board. CSRS employees can also contribute but receive no agency contributions.

Wage Base--(See Maximum Taxable Wage Base.)

Windfall Elimination Provision (WEP)--This provision of the Social Security law reduces Social Security benefits for employees who have less than 30 years of substantial coverage under Social Security and get a pension from employment not covered by Social Security (for example, a CSRS benefit). [105]

---

[105] http://www.opm.gov/fers_election/html/glossary.htm

Suggested Reading

The books and newsletter I have suggested for reading will provide great benefit to applicants that are unfamiliar with the culture of the federal government and law enforcement in specific.

E-Newsletters and E-Publications

The beauty of the e-publications I have listed is they are free and provide tremendous insight about their specific topics. All of the listed e-publications represent a great opportunity to gain insight into current federal law enforcement topics. Wow, imagine the surprise of an interviewer if you ask him an intelligent relevant job question; a question that you derived from reading one of the following e-publications.

FedSmith.com is an information portal for sources of information affecting the federal community. The site provides links to daily news headlines, original articles from their writers, a job posting board and quick links to pages of interest to the federal community and those interested in the Federal Government's activities. They use their extensive experience in working with the federal sector to provide stories of interest throughout the week and to compile a list of organizations and sites with a wealth of information.[106] This is a great Web site, highly recommended. I use it almost daily while at my federal job.

HSToday.us, the HS stands for Homeland Security and this Web site provides comprehensive insights and analysis on homeland security topics. They publish a monthly magazine by the same name, HSToday. Great articles and a terrific way for the novice to get up to speed on some of the issues facing federal and state law enforcement.

CBP Today formerly known as Customs today is the official newsletter of the Bureau of Customs and Border Protection. The link will bring you to all of the archived articles. In 2008, it is being renamed to Frontline and will be published quarterly instead of the previous bimonthly editions.

Books

An agency's law enforcement officers usually do Job interviews. During an interview, applicants must draw upon their own experiences through thoughts and memories while responding to questions. The books I recommend reading will provide you a similar frame of reference as the interviewer as well as an understanding of the mindset of a police officer. It would be misguided to think that all officers have read the selections I have spotlighted or to believe there are no other books worthy of making the list. However, it is very likely that every officer has been trained based on the principles and thoughts written in the recommended books.

---

[106]http://www.fedsmith.com/about/

The more you can think and articulate thoughts like the officers that are interviewing you, the better your chances of getting the job. Secondly, purely from a professional and officer safety and survival standpoint, it will only benefit you to read these books. I have linked the Amazon.com editorial reviews and descriptive web pages to the recommended selections. The book list is in alphabetical order by title. Tactical Edge: Surviving High-Risk Patrol and Street Survival: Tactics for Armed Encounters, are only sold to police officers through the publisher at CalibrePress.com, however, you may also find them at a library or as a second hand book from Amazon.com.

- The Calling: The Making of a Veteran Cop
- On Combat: The Psychology and Physiology of Deadly Conflict in War and in Peace
- On Killing: The Psychological Cost of Learning to Kill in War and Society
- Tactical Advantage: A Definitive Study Of Personal Small-Arms Tactics
- Tactical Edge: Surviving High-Risk Patrol
- Training at the Speed of Life, Vol. 1: The Definitive Textbook for Police and Military Reality Based Training
- Street Survival : Tactics For Armed Encounters
- Verbal Judo: The Gentle Art of Persuasion